AF478146

The Critical Theory of Robert W. Cox

International Political Economy Series

General Editor: Timothy M. Shaw, Professor and Director, Institute of International Relations, The University of the West Indies, Trinidad & Tobago

Titles include:

Anthony Leysens
THE CRITICAL THEORY OF ROBERT W. COX
Fugitive or Guru?

International Political Economy Series
Series Standing Order ISBN 978–0–333–71708–0 hardcover
Series Standing Order ISBN 978–0–333–71110–1 paperback
(*outside North America only*)

You can receive future titles in this series as they are published by placing a standing order. Please contact your bookseller or, in case of difficulty, write to us at the address below with your name and address, the title of the series and one of the ISBNs quoted above.

Customer Services Department, Macmillan Distribution Ltd, Houndmills, Basingstoke, Hampshire RG21 6XS, England

The Critical Theory of Robert W. Cox

Fugitive or Guru?

Anthony Leysens
Senior Lecturer, Department of Political Science
University of Stellenbosch, South Africa

First published 2008 by
PALGRAVE MACMILLAN
Houndmills, Basingstoke, Hampshire RG21 6XS and
175 Fifth Avenue, New York, N.Y. 10010
Companies and representatives throughout the world

PALGRAVE MACMILLAN is the global academic imprint of the Palgrave Macmillan division of St. Martin's Press, LLC and of Palgrave Macmillan Ltd. Macmillan® is a registered trademark in the United States, United Kingdom and other countries. Palgrave is a registered trademark in the European Union and other countries.

ISBN-13: 978–0–230–22479–7   hardback
ISBN-10: 0–230–22479–2   hardback

This book is printed on paper suitable for recycling and made from fully managed and sustained forest sources. Logging, pulping and manufacturing processes are expected to conform to the environmental regulations of the country of origin.

A catalogue record for this book is available from the British Library.

Library of Congress Cataloging-in-Publication Data
Leysens, Anthony.
    The critical theory of Robert W. Cox : Fugitive or guru? / Anthony
        Leysens.
          p. cm. – (International political economy series)
    Includes bibliographical references and index.
    ISBN 0–230–22479–2 (alk. paper)
    1. International relations. 2. World politics. 3. Cox, Robert W.,
    1926 – Political and social views. I. Title.

    JZ1305.L49 2008
    327.101–dc22   2008016418

10   9   8   7   6   5   4   3   2   1
17   16   15   14   13   12   11   10   09   08

Printed and bound in Great Britain by
CPI Antony Rowe, Chippenham and Eastbourne

Contents

List of Abbreviations

AFL-CIO	American Federation of Labour – Congress of Industrial Organisations
ANC	African National Congress
CCT	Coxian Critical Theory
CT	Critical Theory
DRC	Development Research Centre
GATT	General Agreement on Tariffs & Trade
GPE	Global Political Economy
IILS	International Institute for Labour Studies
ILO	International Labour Organisation
IMF	International Monetary Fund
IPE	International Political Economy
IR	International Relations
ISA	International Studies Association
MNC	Multinational Corporation
MUNS	Multilateralism in the UN System
NGO	Non-Governmental Organisation
NIEO	New International Economic Order
OECD	Organisation for Economic Co-operation and Development
PPWO	Production, Power and World Order
UNCTAD	UN Conference on Trade and Development
UNU	United Nations University
USSR	Union of Soviet Socialist Republics
WB	World Bank
WOMP	World Order Models Project

Preface

History is rarely kind to social scientists. In Machines as the Measure of Man, historian Michael Adas mines three centuries of the forgotten one-time "giants" of European social science to uncover the banal, self-congratulatory images that rich white people have had about their place in the world. Adas is one of the few people living who has ever read so much old social science. Today's students read maybe one economist from the 18th century, and only two or three from the 19th. Scholars of international relations are even less well favored. In 1939, E. H. Carr had to introduce his readers to the name of W. T. Stead, the most widely read British writer on world affairs just 40 years before. The book in which Carr makes that introduction, *The Twenty Years Crisis*, is probably the only mid-20th century book read by most international relations graduate students today.

In 2050, few of the international relations scholars writing today will still be read. Robert W. Cox will be one of them and his *Power, Production, and World Order* may be one of the few books in the field still read more than 70 years after its publication.

Cox's place in the history of the field will be secure even without the publication of Anthony Leysens' book, but Leysens' book will help this generation, and the next, understand the particularity of Cox's vision.

We will come to understand that vision in its proper context.

In the 1980s, when Cox first came into prominence as a major theorist of international relations, many of his admirers – including some who had read him carefully and who understood him well – very deliberately lumped his views together with a wide range of theories with which Cox's ideas were only marginally connected. Clarity – and some might argue, a degree of intellectual integrity – was sacrificed to the more pressing goal of creating and preserving space in the academy for the whole range of what was called "dissident" scholarship in international relations.

In the process, Cox's self-described "critical" theory became lumped together with a range of work that leant heavily on the

"Critical Theory" of the Frankfurt School, especially the work done after its leading exponents came to the United States.

Leysens has carefully restored the intellectual distance between Cox's analysis and other forms of critical theory. He has done so by providing a very close reading of Cox's work and a careful investigation of the actual sources of Cox's concepts, both in the works that he cites and in the immediate intellectual milieux in which Cox developed his ideas – both within the United Nations system and in the academy. Leysens' contrasting analysis of the role of Frankfurt School ideas in current international relations scholarship further clarifies the distinctiveness of Cox's contribution.

Like Antonio Gramsci's prison writings, most of what Cox has written after his turn to academic life was written *für ewig*, for all time, or, at least, it was meant to be of use for many years, something like the chair built by the Shaker who knew that he may die tomorrow but that what he built might be used for 100 years.

Cox writes this way not because he considers himself a better craftsman than the self-described international relations "scientists" who hope that their work will be transcended by "better" theories. Cox writes this way because his purpose is to uncover the fundamental sources of contemporary international relations – the forces that gave the contemporary world order, and the 19th century order out of which it grew, its specific form. That is why Cox will still be read in 50 years the way we still read Carr, today: to gain insight into the origins and dynamics of a world order that may have passed, but that, nevertheless, gave rise to the world in which we live.

Leysens' study helps us see Cox's purpose and the power of his ideas.

We seem to live in a time that demands a kind of critical realism; Leysens helps us build on the critical realism that Cox has already created.

Craig N. Murphy
Radcliffe Institute of Advanced Study

Acknowledgments

To start with, I wish to extend my sincere appreciation and thanks to Robert Cox, who agreed to read and provide me with written comments on the draft chapters of the book, as I completed them. His invaluable input focused on matters of fact and clarification, and not on 'correctness' of interpretation. For the latter, I alone am responsible. The final text has gained much from his recollections, and for this I am indebted to him.

I am greatly indebted to Pierre du Toit, at Stellenbosch University's Political Science Department, who, over many years, has been (and continuous to be) a mentor and steadfast colleague.

Thanks are also due to Tim Shaw, International Political Economy Series editor, who believed in the merits of the book and greatly facilitated the process towards its publication.

I am grateful to Craig Murphy for agreeing to write a preface to the book which encapsulates the significance and the endurance of Robert Cox's work.

Audun Solli, a talented graduate student, upon hearing of the book when it was still in project form, immediately offered his assistance. He undertook the bulk of the research work for the section in Chapter 6 which focuses on the 'followers' of Cox. I benefitted greatly from our discussions and incorporated many of his analytical insights. A particular word of thanks is due to him for his unwavering dedication and willingness to go the extra mile without any financial compensation. The usual disclaimers apply.

Thanks are due to Hennie Kotzé (Dean) and Amanda Gouws (chair of department) who arranged the financial assistance which enabled me to devote an entire semester to the book.

Finally, and most importantly, much love and appreciation to Lisa, who never ceases to encourage, inspire and support me, and to Benjamin, Daniel and Jean-Louis. In as much as they had to share and spare me during the writing of this book, the final product belongs to them, as much as it belongs to me.

1
Why a Book on the Critical Theory of Robert W. Cox?

Introduction

The work of the Canadian historian and political economist, Robert W. Cox, goes back some thirty to fifty years (if one includes the time when he was an international civil servant at the International Labour Organisation). The value of his contribution to, specifically, the fields of International Relations (IR) and International Political Economy (IPE),[1] is widely recognised. Coxian Critical Theory (CCT) has been one major source (the other being the work of Susan Strange) of inspiration for what Cohen (2007) identifies as the British school of IPE. Although there are less adherents of CCT in the 'American school of IPE', Murphy (2007: 7) points out that a recent survey of IR scholars in the United States (US) found that Cox's name is among the top twenty-five names cited as having '...had the greatest impact on the field in the last two decades'.

Recognition and acknowledgment has come in various forms. An edited volume by Stephen Gill and James Mittelman (1997) in honour of Robert and Jessie Cox includes contributions from a number of prominent scholars on the themes of innovation and transformation in international studies. The journal, *New Political Economy*, in its last issue of 1999, interviewed Manuel Castells, Robert Cox and Immanuel Wallerstein to reflect on the millennium transition. Randall Germain, Ankie Hoogvelt and Michael Kenny (who conducted the interviews) motivated the selection of Castells, Cox and Wallerstein as follows: 'Our choice was restricted, for there are not many internationally reputed and theoretically inclined social scientists today who have the boldness of vision, the appetite for transdisciplinary thought and the intellectual fortitude necessary for sustained theoretical coherence of the kind that characterised the foundational work of our nineteenth century forebears' (Hoogvelt *et al.*, 1999: 379).

In 2007, the International Studies Association (ISA) convention included two panels to assess and reconsider the contributions of Cox (and long-time collaborator, Jeffrey Harrod) which culminated in the publication of Cox's seminal *Production, Power, and World Order: Social Forces in the Making of History* (1987) (PPWO) and Harrod's *Power, Production and the Unprotected Worker* (1987). Reviewing PPWO, Strange's (1988a: 269), introductory remarks encapsulated the importance of this volume, but also hinted at the debate about how Cox should be understood (and read) which was to follow: 'Books that mark turning-points in perceptions of international affairs, that succeed in redirecting thought and argument in quite new directions, are rare indeed. It is a fair guess that this is one, for all that it is not a particularly easy read.'

Why has CCT managed to remain on the theoretical agenda of IR/IPE?[2] Why, over the years, has it attracted a school of followers? These questions will be expanded on in the ensuing chapters. Nevertheless, some initial observations are warranted to point to the endurance of, what I call, Cox's core theoretical framework. Normatively, it provides a non-mainstream alternative to those who subscribe to a worldview, which emphasises social equity (across identities such as gender, race, ethnicity and class), civilisational diversity (or plurality), and environmental sustainability. It also critically focuses on the potential of multilateralism to act as a means to achieving these ends.[3]

Analytically, CCT offers a comprehensive framework, which is aimed at the understanding of social change. To achieve this, the framework incorporates the dynamic interaction and mutual influence between three layers[4]: social forces, forms of state, and world orders. Social forces (within state-society complexes or interacting with political authorities) are regarded as a potential catalyst to bring about the transformation of forms of state and world order.[5] Finally, CCT works with the assumption that ideas and the material world are connected. This leads to a 'reflexive' approach to theory (theories are linked to context and subject) and the notion of intersubjective understandings ('social facts' or 'constructs' in the terminology of the constructivists who came after Cox).

Coxian Critical Theory thus focuses on the development of various state forms in response to changes in the way social forces relate to production,[6] and in response to changing world orders. Forms of state, in turn, influence production modes and social forces, as well as world orders. In contemporary terms and foreseen by Cox (1981, 1987), the autonomy of the state has been reduced by what he termed 'the internationalisation of production' (today, the globalisation of production). It is interesting that Strange, who is regarded as having prioritised the financial structure in her understanding of IPE, also accepted the importance of production. Perhaps she was influenced by her reading of Cox's PPWO when she noted that changes in the production structure are likely to be accompanied by changes '…in the distribution of social and political power, and sometimes the nature of the state and the authority over the market' (Strange, 1988b: 62).

The dynamics of CCT function within the parameters of specific historical structures, which can be hegemonic or non-hegemonic. A hegemonic historical structure is characterised by a 'fit' between ideas, institutions and material capabilities. Attainment of hegemony depends on both coercion and consensus. When contradictions arise between these three forces, the 'fit' comes apart and the potential for transformation (within the limits of the possible) and a counter-hegemonic challenge presents itself. The utility and application of this framework is illustrated in rich historical detail in PPWO. The book focuses, among others, on the *pax brittanica* as an example of a historical structure.

Briefly, the rise of the industrial and merchant classes, and the consequent appearance of the industrial working class (social forces) in England led to a new form of state (liberal). This change in state form impacted on the world order of the time, leading to increased rivalry (military and industrial) between the major European powers. The *idea*, which underpinned the liberal state form, emphasised the separation of politics and economics (in theory). Poverty was assumed to be a personal responsibility (1834 Poor Law Reform). At the world order level, hegemony was maintained by England's *material capabilities* (maritime and industrial dominance) to manage the balance of power in Europe and to maintain open trade and commercial access.

Although there were no *institutions* comparable to the International Monetary Fund (IMF) and World Bank (WB), the City of London was responsible for maintaining a gold exchangeable currency system to facilitate trade (gold standard). The *contradictions* in this historical structure arose from the social costs that accompanied the liberal state form in England. Pressure by organised labour and sympathetic industrialists led to the enactment of social safety net laws and (in Polanyian terms) the re-embedding of the market into society (the welfarist-nationalist state form) (Cox, 1987: 123–47).

I propose that the 'nuts and bolts' of CCT continue to provide the analyst with a useful heuristic and explanatory tool with which we can enhance our understanding of the contemporary world order. The major challenges for those who want to apply CCT comprehensively are located in critically understanding the nuances in Cox's thought, its origins and the development thereof, and his historical method or 'historicism' (Mittelman, 1998). The latter, for Cox, refers to the ability to insert one's mind into the mentality of people living and coping with their material environment. Murphy (2007: 2), in a timely article which reviews the 'promise of critical IR', senses that students are still instructed to regard Cox's seminal 1981 and 1983 articles as the start of IR's critical turn. I will attempt to illustrate in what follows, that Murphy's 'hunch' is correct, but that Cox's work is incorrectly associated with the Frankfurt School of CT and Habermas.

Issues and objectives

An inspection of introductory and advanced texts in IR/IPE reveals that Cox's work has not escaped a favourite pursuit of theoretically minded scholars in these fields. The attempt to 'place' or categorise those who have made it their goal to contribute to the development of theory is probably as old as the founding of the first academic department dedicated to the study of International Politics in Aberystwyth. Because he is an 'outsider' to the traditional academic path (via Political Science and Economics) which IR/IPE scholars usually follow, Cox's contribution is difficult to categorise. In fact, I will argue that his work cannot be 'moulded' into the traditional mainstream paradigms of IR/IPE (Marxism, neo-Realism and Liberalism).[7] Michael Schechter (2002: 3), in an excellent chapter which sets the stage for Cox to engage with some of his critics, notes that 'Much ink has been spilled on trying to classify Cox's work.' This book is not another attempt to do so.

Rather, my intention is to address three issues. Firstly, I aim to address the problem of the incorrect 'placing' and 'linking' of Cox's approach. This relates to, on the one hand, the representation of his work as Marxist, neo-Marxist[8] (for instance, Baylis and Smith, 2001; Brown, 1992; Jackson and Sørensen, 1999) or neo-Gramscian (Germain and Kenny, 1998)[9] and, on the other hand, to the linking or association of Cox with the Frankfurt School of Critical Theory (CT)[10] and/or more specifically with Jürgen Habermas. This linkage, in turn, leads to the association of CCT with a group of scholars who are regarded as having played an instrumental role in the launching of the 'critical turn' in IR/IPE. Thus, Cox is placed in the company of Richard Ashley, Mark Hoffman, Andrew Linklater, and Mark Neufeld who to a greater or lesser extent draw on, or have been inspired by CT (I will elaborate shortly). The question arises, therefore, as to why these associations are made, and why they persist.[11]

The second issue relates to the title of this book. In the book review of PPWO referred to above, Strange (1988a: 269–70) concludes that Cox is a '...loner, a fugitive from intellectual camps of victory, both Marxist and liberal'. I propose that Cox, in the first instance, was a fugitive from 'practice' rather than theory. Having 'lived through' the experience of being subjected to a hegemonic imposition of 'common sense' thinking (Murphy and Tooze, 1991) at the ILO, he was perhaps led to the theories of those who could assist his own understanding (theory) of that experience. That experience, in it itself, would lead one to be cautious of 'intellectual camps of victory'. In a review essay of Susan Strange's work, Cox had this to say on the attributes of the loner, 'Loners live on the margins. They may have an unconventional background...Loners tend to define their own issues and their own conceptual frameworks...One risk for a loner is inadvertently to become a guru...' (Cox, 1992c: 178–9).

The analysis which follows will illustrate the intellectual process which led to the development of a 'fugitive' theoretical framework, but it will end of with a 'snapshot' of those who have attempted to follow or were inspired by CCT. Theoretical innovators usually attract a following, and CCT has been no exception. However, how have the followers of Coxian historicism utilised the insights and guidelines of the guru? I distinguish between those who give a nod in CCT's direction, those who selectively incorporate aspects of it, and those who attempt to comprehensively apply it. Furthermore, what do these attempts tell us about CCT? I will deal with this issue in the last chapter which is a 'working' conclusion in the sense that it extrapolates from the main findings, the 'followers' and, offers some suggestions for the way forward.

In the last section of Chapter 6, I address the future of CCT and its potential as a 'bridging' framework. Recently, some voices have been raised who argue that the time has come for the start of a conversation between critical and empiricist approaches in IPE. For instance, Cohen's (2007)[12] thought provoking article on the 'transatlantic divide' in IPE, as represented by the American and British schools. In the article, he discusses the differences between the two schools, the contexts (historically) within which they emerged, the more well known scholars who can be regarded as representative of the two 'factions', and the directions in which both schools moved. The major difference can be summarised as lying in the 'empiricism' and the deductive-nomological model of the American school and the critical interpretative approach of the British school which prioritises historical and social context (Cohen, 2007: 198, 216).

Cohen concludes that the divide has resulted in the emergence of a 'new dialogue of the deaf', but proposes that both schools have much to offer to each other. He ends of eclectically, by suggesting that 'synthesis' may be the way forward, '…why not seek to take the best from both, for their mutual gain?' (Cohen, 2007: 217). The question which Cohen's article leaves us with is, how can this be done? I conclude that CCT offers those who are interested in bridging the divide, a potential way forward.[13] The result of such an undertaking may result in an approach which is 'critically empiricist'. My goal is modest, it is to point out why and how CCT could lend itself as a vehicle for moving forward to a critically empiricist framework. I will not attempt to develop such a framework here.

Elaborating on the 'Association' and 'Bridging' questions

In this section, I will briefly amplify and motivate, in particular, the rationale behind the question which focuses on CCT's association with the Critical Theory of the Frankfurt School (CT) and scholars in IR/IPE who have been inspired by it in their own work. I will also expand on and provide a basis for why I think CCT has the potential to act as bridge between the empiricist and interpretivist schools.

Several authors make the association between CCT, CT and the critical turn in IR/IPE, in one way or another. They include Brown (1994), Devetak (1996), George (1989 and 1994), Hoffman (1987), Linklater (1992), Neufeld (1993a) and Smith (1995). For instance, Brown (1994: 213) states that 'A number of critical theorists in international relations make at least a partial claim to be Critical Theorists...employing some of these notions in their work. Robert Cox uses Habermasian ideas in his contrast between "problem-solving" and "critical" theory, and Andrew Linklater's approach to critical international theory explicitly employs the notion of knowledge-constituting interests.' (Brown, 1994: 213).

Devetak (1996) while discussing the role of CT in IR, sets out the assumptions of the Frankfurt School (particularly as related to the work of Max Horkheimer and Habermas) and then goes on to link these to Ashley and Linklater (justifiably), but also to Cox. He goes on to refer to '...Cox's Horkheimer-like distinction between problem-solving and critical theories' and concludes that 'The debt to Horkheimer in Cox's assessment of problem-solving and critical theories is plain to see.' (Devetak, 1996: 149, 151).

In an article on the 'third debate' in IR, George (1989: 274) notes that, 'Cox's emancipatory perspective, derived from Frankfurt School sources, has been one of the most significant theoretical influences within the third debate.' Later, in an excellent volume which reviews the state of theory in IR, George (1994) discusses the contributions of Ashley, Cox, Linklater, Hoffman and Rengger to critical theory in IR. In doing so, he obviously assumes that they have something in common. What is the common denominator which has led him to group them together? According to him, it is the influence of Habermas, which is most discernible in the work of Ashley (George, 1994: 171).

Hoffman (1987) makes the strongest case for linking CT with CCT. He identifies a number of authors who he regards as representative of the critical turn in IR, viz. Cox, Ashley and Linklater. Cox is viewed as being the closest to the Frankfurt School. Hoffman (1987: 237) qualifies this linkage by stating that Cox 'draws implicitly on the links between interests and knowledge that are central to the Frankfurt School', and that Cox's view on the nature of theory 'has important similarities with the work of the Frankfurt School.' He also observes that Cox's work 'may owe more' to Vico and Gramsci, than to Horkheimer and Habermas.

However, in a footnote (Hoffman, 1987: 247, footnote 30) he again 'pushes' the connection between Cox and Habermas, when he criticises Kubalkova and Cruickshank (1986) for exaggerating Cox's position on Habermas. Their comment in this regard (also in a footnote) is worth noting in full: 'Cox…refers to neither of the two generations of the Frankfurt School and in fact mentions Habermas as a theorist irrelevant for an understanding of international behaviour' (Kubalkova and Cruickshank, 1986: 181, footnote 9). To this Hoffman (1987: 247, footnote 30) replies that Cox does not regard Habermas as 'irrelevant for an understanding of international behaviour' but that he criticises him for not taking into account 'the implications of different forms of state/civil society relationships.'

Linklater (1992: 91) while discussing the merits of the Frankfurt School for a 'critical-theoretical point of view' in IR cites Ashley and Cox as being representative of the critical challenge to neo-Realism. He elaborates, 'When Cox and Ashley struck the first blow for critical theory in the early 1980s, they challenged the contention that knowledge should be constituted solely by a "technical interest" in control', and concludes, 'The details of the argument were set out by Habermas…' thereby suggesting that Ashley, and Cox were inspired by Habermas.

Finally, the following comments by Smith (1995: 24) are noteworthy. In an overview of the development of theory in IR and under the heading of 'The Post-Positivist Debate', he identifies a number of challengers to the dominant paradigm in IR (Realism). One such challenge, he observes, comes from critical theory (as represented by Cox, Hoffman and Linklater), 'For critical theorists, knowledge of the world is always to be understood within a context of interests, following on from the pioneering work of the Frankfurt School, most notably Jürgen Habermas.' (Smith, 1995: 24). For these theorists critical theory should take the place of 'problem-solving positivism'.

The excerpts and comments above are indicative of an incorrect linking of Cox with CT and the critical IR school (those who admit to being inspired by CT and Habermas). They are also not accurate reflections of his thinking on (classical) realism and positivism (empiricism). This association continues today, albeit with some notable exceptions (see for instance, Falk, 1997; Mittelman, 1998 and Wyn Jones, 2001).

I now turn to a brief elaboration on the potential of CCT to act as a bridge between critical and empiricist approaches. The point that positivism (problem-solving theory) and critical theory (of the Coxian variety) can potentially be used in tandem is made unambiguously by Cox. For instance, 'Regularities in human activities may indeed be observed…and thus the positivist approach can be fruitful within defined historical limits' (Cox, 1986: 244). In his differentiation between the actor-interactions approach of positivism and the historical structures approach, Cox (1989b: 38) indicates that he does not view them in an either/or manner, 'The structural approach is not so much an alternative to the actor-interactions approach as a logical priority to it.' Drawing a distinction between the positivist ('incremental change') approach to the study of international organisations and the 'structural-critical' approach, he observes that '…some combination may be appropriate' (Cox, 1997a: xvi–xvii). Finally, Sinclair (1996: 6) in a review chapter of Cox's contribution to IR theory, concludes: 'Problem-solving and critical theory are not necessarily mutually exclusive. They may be understood to address different concerns or levels within one overall story.'

These points are (again) confirmed by Cox in the *New Political Economy* 'conversation' with Randall Germain. He emphasises the importance of focusing on something specific by isolating it temporarily. Thereafter one has to connect it with other aspects that are related to it. This requires a pulling back' to critically ascertain how the specific relates to the whole and whether it helps one to understand the dynamics of transformation. The manner in which this may be attempted has been misunderstood by readers of his work and his comments concerning this need to be cited in full:[14] 'This problem brings us to the distinction I have made between problem-solving and critical theory. Some people have read this to mean that I am against problem-solving theory, which was not at all my point. The important consideration for me is that problem-solving theory is useful within its limits, but that one needs to be aware that, in a period of rather important and significant structural change, these limits are a constraint that prevents you from seeing where you can go and what sorts of problems you are facing.' (Cox, 1999b: 392–3).

Structure

To address the questions outlined above, a comprehensive analysis of Cox's English language publications (he has also published in French) was undertaken. As a source list, the complete bibliography of Cox's work until 1995 (provided in Cox with Sinclair, 1996) was used. Publications by Cox after 1995 were sourced from the *Social Sciences Citation Index*. The aim is to provide an accurate intellectual biography or 'genealogy', which focuses on major influences, epistemology and the ontology of his core theoretical framework. The results are discussed in Chapter 2 which focuses on early influences and development of thought. The core theoretical framework of CCT is the theme of Chapter 3, in which I also refer to his later work on multilateralism and civilisations.

The next two chapters serve as comparative points of reference. To compare CCT with the Frankfurt School of Critical Theory (CT), Chapter 4 offers an overview of CT's origin, development and assumptions. The next chapter focuses on the work of four scholars (Ashley, Linklater, Hoffman and Neufeld) who have attempted to incorporate CT into IR/IPE theory and with whom Cox is often associated. I will attempt to show how they have used CT in their own work and why they regard Cox as being representative of the 'critical turn' in IR/IPE. When necessary, in Chapters 4 and 5, references will be made to CCT for comparative purposes. Chapter 6, presents the main findings, incorporates a brief review of the work of some of the followers of CCT and, (in the spirit of CCT) offers some suggestions towards the realisation of a potential critical empiricist approach.

2
Influences, Context, and Theoretical Development

Introduction

It is difficult to present the development of Cox's thinking and those who have influenced him in neatly contained packages, because he has incorporated insights from a variety of sources during the process. This does not mean, however, that there is no consistency in his worldview and thinking. For instance, the discussion, which follows, shows that there is a constant concern with broader historical contextualisation, even during the 'positivist phase'. In this regard, the major concepts and assumptions of what I regard as Cox's core theoretical framework, his work after PPWO, as well as his perspectives on knowledge, ontology, theory and method form an essential component of the 'early years' analysis. However, in order to do justice to the 'genealogy' metaphor, the approach followed in this chapter and the next is a chronological one. I regard the publication of PPWO, in 1987, as the end of a process that culminated in the establishment of the core theoretical framework. The analysis is therefore divided into pre-1987 and post-1987 publications.

The chronological approach facilitates one of the major goals of this book, to trace the development (no linear progression is assumed!) of Cox's thinking through a review analysis of some of his major publications, and by pointing to contextual and scholarly influences.

This chapter, reviews in some detail, the development of Cox's pre-1987 thinking and how this contributed to the emergence of core assumptions. This is done through an exegesis of his publications. The purpose is to provide the reader with an insight into who Cox drew on during the process of the development of his own explanatory framework, and also into the context within which this process unfolded. This is an important precursor to our consideration of whether the linking of Cox's work with the Frankfurt School, and the placing thereof within a CT of IR approach (together with other scholars) is warranted. Furthermore, is this linking based on an accurate reading and close assessment of his work?

Early context and influences

The development of Robert Cox's critical perspective was substantially shaped by his time spent at the ILO in Geneva, Switzerland. The content of what was to become CCT, was influenced by his study of history (at McGill University, Canada) and the scholars he read over the years. Cox himself made the observation, in an interview with Randall Germain (1999b: 380), that the restrictions which were placed on his intellectual autonomy by the bureaucratic ethos prevalent at the ILO (particularly during his later years there), contributed much to his thinking on change and the need for critical theory. Hoogvelt *et al.* (1999: 380) conclude, 'Surely a case of "I think where I am"?' His early experience with bureaucracy would also be reflected in his pessimism later on in life as to whether critical thinking and a focus on change could take place from within large organisations (more particularly, in reference to the United Nations and universities) (Cox, 1999b: 391, 398).

Towards the end of his time at McGill University, Cox was offered and accepted an invitation to join the ILO (the organisation had located itself on campus during the war years) in Geneva. His career at the ILO was to span some twenty-five years, from 1948 to 1972. From his early university years (he earned a Masters in History, and graduated with top honours) he took with him, among others, the work of E.H. Carr and George Sorel, two scholars who had very different views on the state. Carr would be credited with returning the study of international relations to the *realpolitik* of the state. Sorel, on the other hand, saw the state as an entity that needed to be eliminated in its modern form. Cox would consistently retain, in his own work, Carr's emphasis on the relationship between industrialisation, the nature of the state, ideas, and change at the world order level. He was greatly impressed by Carr's approach to not separate 'levels of analysis' and to focus on structural change. Sorel taught him '...that you could take some things from Marxism without swallowing the whole package' as well as a critical disposition towards positivism as a method for the understanding of social behaviour. Crucially for an understanding of Cox's historical method, as we will see, Sorel understood historical materialism to be '...the relationship between mentalities and material conditions of existence' (Cox, 1996b: 27–8).

During his university years, together with Carr and Sorel, there were others that shaped Cox's thinking on the historical method. He viewed 'historicism' (an emerging concept at this stage) as an approach that was superior to studies that are constrained by time and space. Cox recalls that during his first year as a history student he received a book prize and chose Oswald Spengler's *Decline of the West*, George Sorel's *Reflections on Violence*, and James Burham's *The Machiavellians*. He views these books as reflecting interests that have '...been sustained and developed' (personal communication, 31 March 2007). Spengler would later (during the post-1987 period) rekindle his interest in the notion of civilisations and what lies behind them.[1]

The historian, R.G. Collingwood (with Sorel) shaped Cox's thinking on what he would later call 'intersubjectivity'. Collingwood's notion that the study of history required 'rethinking the thought of the past' (combined with Sorel's ideas on the link between consciousness and existence) led Cox to view the interaction between what we experience and how we interpret and react to that experience as a crucial component of any historicist attempt to explain (political and social) change. Herein lies one of the greatest challenges to those who want to apply Cox's method of historicism. It is through the social practices and institutions which people collectively devise that they deal with the demands imposed on them by the 'material conditions of their existence'. From Collingwood, Cox would later (after leaving the ILO in 1972 and taking up a position at Columbia University, City of New York) return to Giambattista Vico, and on to Antonio Gramsci. These early influences, taken together with the work of Fernand Braudel, Ibn Khaldun and Karl Polanyi form the backbone of his historical mode of understanding.

The International Labour Organisation phase

In one of his first publications (a book review), while at the ILO, Cox (1953) emphasises that we cannot look at ideas in isolation from the historical context in which they originated and evolved. Writing on the 'idea of international labour regulation', he points out that the notion of regulating labour can only be understood as the outcome of power relations between social forces, changes in production, changes in the form of state, and changes in ideas during nineteenth century England. Here already, his view of history as a 'mode of understanding' and not just the study of events related to a specific time and space, is reflected. Tracing the development and acceptance of international labour regulation, Cox (1953: 44–6) shows how this was in the interest of industrial employers and the state at a time when European states were becoming increasingly nationalist in their outlook. After the suppression of the working class challenge in mid-century, industrial employers like Daniel Legrand propagated for international labour regulation (agreed among the first industrialised states), to prevent the emergence of 'class war'.

Thinking of whose interests would be served by this 'idea', Cox (1953: 44) concludes that the policies of national governments to improve the lot of workers, would be curtailed by an international agreement, the effect of which would be to aid the industrialists in resisting the demands for domestic change. These demands intensified during the last decades of the nineteenth century and the years leading up to World War I, when the increase in the industrial power of organised labour required incorporation, not suppression. What was needed was state intervention to protect labour from foreign competition, as well as the enactment of social security policies. Thus, changes in the power of social forces related to production, led to a change in the form of state (nationalist-corporatist). At the international level, it was in the interest of the major industrialised states (with Britain leading the field) to agree to international regulation in order to prevent international working class solidarity. It was also a strategy to remove the contestation of labour standards out of the international arena. Furthermore, it was compatible with further industrial expansion and nationalism.

This early article reflects the kind of thinking which Cox would refine over the years. Ideas are not isolated from events; we need to ask whose interests they serve, how and why? How are they related to the social events of the time, and why did they not evolve elsewhere? (Cox, 1953: 41).

During the next fifteen years, Cox's work initially reflected a more positivist methodology, and focused on leadership and decision-making in international organisations. For this, his experiences at the ILO were important. During this period, however, he still combined empiricism with an eye for the constraints imposed by broader context, and a willingness to be critical of the bureaucratic ethos prevalent in international organisations (again, particularly influenced by his position at the ILO). During the years that David Morse was director-general of the ILO (1948–1970), Cox felt himself able to exercise the kind of critical role within the ILO, which enabled him to stay on for the length of time that he did. His major problem with the organisation was the espousal of a form of labour-management relations (tripartism) which was Euro-American centric, and which was accepted as universal in form and not historically contingent. He encapsulates his feelings about this period as follows, 'I found myself in the moral position of the anthropologist – a participant observer of my new tribe. I was in it but could not be entirely of it insofar as I reflected upon the sources of the norms it espoused.' (Cox, 1996b: 22).

The time span of Cox's career at the ILO virtually coincides with David Morse's. He was Morse's 'principal staff officer', and then went on to become chief of the ILO's Program and Planning Division. During the latter part of his career at the ILO, Morse appointed him as director of the International Institute for Labour Studies (IILS). His long stay at the ILO (albeit as 'participant observer') was undoubtedly facilitated by the fact that he and Morse got along, and that the latter was prepared to allow criticism and autonomous thinking. Cox (1996b: 23–4) recalls that Morse had no problem with criticism from within and even regarded it as a healthy state of affairs. Nevertheless, this was still subject to his having power over the practical implications of such criticism, '…the critical faculty had only powers of expression, not of decision'. In contrast, Cox experienced Morse's successor, Clarence Wilfred Jenks, as 'frequently overbearing' (Cox, 1977: 436, 444).

While at the ILO, Cox managed to take time off to do work of a more academic nature (teaching and research). In 1964, he spent a year at the Graduate Institute of International Studies in Geneva. During this time, he delivered an inaugural lecture on the ideologies of international organisations and also wrote a paper with the title, 'The Executive Head'. The paper, which dealt with the leadership challenges in international organisations, ruffled many bureaucratic feathers among the 'conformists' at the ILO. Presumably, they subscribed to the Western idea of labour-management relations. Cox remembers the incident as one that brought him into disrepute with the organisational ideologists, 'From then on, I was a controversial figure in an organizational milieu that put a premium on conformity.' (Cox, 1996b: 23).

As noted above, Cox's 'positivist phase' was very much in evidence during this time (Sinclair, 1996: 12), but at the same time reflected an ongoing concern with the need for transformation, representivity and inclusiveness in international organisations. For instance, in an article on the potential leadership role of the executive head in transforming an international organisation, he attempts to answer the question whether international organisations are more than just a reflection of the power politics of member states, '...do they influence world politics in their own right?' (Cox, 1969: 318). The 'hypothesis within the hypothesis' is then whether the executive head, 'among possible conversion variables' can be instrumental in converting/transforming an organisation of state-centric multilateralism to one which reflects 'a more integrated international system'. The end result (an integrated international system) would be one where inter-state conflict is addressed via '...higher common interests and the creation of international agencies to promote and regulate them' (Cox, 1969: 319).

In the same article, Cox sources a functionalist view of international organisations from Ernst Haas' *Beyond the Nation-State: Functionalism and International Organization* (1964). He then attempts to augment Haas' framework by focusing on three key aspects of the executive head's relationships; those related to the international bureaucracy, those related to dealings with member states, and those related to interactions with the international system. It is important to note that he emphasises the crucial role played by sub-national groups (domestic forces) who he argues are in a position to influence the foreign policy of their government towards international organisations.[2] This leads him to propose that international organisations need to maintain links with domestic groups within member states who are well disposed to their goals and that, as such, the executive head needs to keep abreast of '...such favorable currents of domestic opinion as present themselves...' (Cox, 1969: 339–40).

The importance of sub-national (domestic) interests to multilateral organisations is something that Cox would return to in his later (post-1987) work. This also shows that, at this time, he already had a view of the state as an entity, which is permeable, as opposed to one, which regards the state in international relations as a 'billiard ball' (the neo-Realist perspective). Furthermore, although he uses Haas' functionalist positivist framework, Cox stresses the importance of the need to always historically contextualise theory. Finally, and bearing in mind the attempt to associate Cox's work with the Frankfurt School of CT, the article has a brief reference to Herbert Marcuse. The reference is made in the context of the need to view the United Nations (UN) as more than the sum of its parts, but also as an organisation behind which there is a fundamental spirit ('essence'), which must come to the fore. Marcuse is referred to (without a publication citation) as someone who is supportive of this notion of a 'real essence' that hides behind a name.

During his final years at the ILO, Morse appointed Cox as director of the IILS. The institute was established (in 1960) with the aim of acting as an independent and critical think tank within the ILO. It was from within the IILS that Cox (together with Jeffrey Harrod, research coordinator at the IILS and a former doctoral student of Cox's) undertook important groundwork in the identification of types (later, modes) of production relations. This took the form of a survey, an independent effort from within the IILS, to determine patterns in industrial relations. The unrevealed goal was to illustrate that the majority of the world's labourers did not belong to the tripartite (state, labour, employers) arrangement which the ILO favoured. The report (Cox, Harrod, *et al.* 1972) became controversial, because it found that the prevalent tripartite labour-management perspective which was the basis of the ILO's *modus operandi*, applied to only 9% of the world's labour force (see also, Cox, 1977: 444). Based on these findings, Cox would later develop his conceptualisation of different types of modes of social relations of production. His collaboration with Harrod culminated in the publication of *Production, Power and World Order* (1987), accompanied by Harrod's volume, *Power, Production and the Unprotected Worker* (1987).

By this time (1972), Cox's thinking had begun to shift towards the idea of hegemony. This was a concept that he related to his own position at the ILO, as well as to the activities of the ILO as a whole. By his own account, this was brought about by the events which played themselves out during 1968; the student riots in France, the

Soviet intervention in Czechoslovakia, and conversations 'with a very few' critical scholars during a visit to the Union of Soviet Socialist Republics (USSR) in the same year. Thinking about these events led him to realise that there were contradictions in the Cold War world, as well as in his own work environment: 'The movements of 1968...revealed that the convictions of Cold War ideology were transparent and fragile. The hiatus between ideology and reality was manifest'. Reflecting on his role at the ILO and IILS at that time, he realised that his work had indirectly contributed to an approach to labour policies that '...reflected the dominant social forces in the rich countries and the world' (Cox, 1996b: 24–6). This resulted in a greater awareness that, from now on, a more encompassing, critical approach would be needed.

Cox's use of the functionalist approach to study international organisations reached a turning point after the publication of *The Anatomy of Influence: Decision Making in International Organization* (1972). The book, the result of a joint effort between himself and Harold Jacobson, with contributions from, among others, Susan Strange and Joseph Nye was completed at the University of Toronto during a year's leave of absence from the ILO. From now on, Cox would re-dedicate himself to the development of the historical mode of understanding perspective. The publication of the book, in 1972, coincided with the tendering of his resignation from the ILO. It was also the year when a graduate student at the University of Toronto introduced him to Gramsci's work. Cox's resignation was sparked by a combination of changes in his thinking and the appointment of the new ILO director-general in 1970, Wilfred Jenks (Cox, 1996d: xiii, 24).

The IILS's ability to fulfill a critical and independent role had always been constrained, even under the directorship of Morse. This can be attributed to the insistence of US representatives that its research role be restricted by close administrative links to the ILO. Nevertheless, during its formative years it '...made modest progress towards perspectives alternative to those of the ILO's official ideology' (Cox, 1977: 444). This modicum of autonomy came to an end under the directorship of Jenks. Cox (1996b: 24) recalls that, 'This was not a person with whom I could maintain a civilized dialogue about our differences.' He regarded Jenks as someone who stood solely and purely in the service of the official ILO line on labour relations. (Cox, 1977: 445).

Apart from the difference in management style between Morse and Jenks, the latter also insisted that any publications that emanated from the ILO and IILS had to pass through him for approval. Accordingly, publications, which did not exercise the right of freedom of speech 'responsibly', could be vetoed in terms of what Jenks called his right of *nihil obstat*. When Jenks attempted to exercise this right with respect to Cox's chapter in the *Anatomy of Influence*, Cox tendered his letter of resignation (12 June 1972). A full account of his reasons is footnoted (note 49) in the article 'Labor and Hegemony' (1977). The article also refers to Jenks' management style, during his brief tenure as director-general (he died in 1973), as 'absolutist' and based on the 'doctrine of tripartism'.

Academia: Refining the historical mode of understanding

After leaving the ILO, Cox accepted a position at Columbia University (City of New York) as 'Professor of International Organization'. However, at that time, his intellectual development had led him away from the positivist functionalist approach to international organisations: 'I had abandoned the concept of international organisation in favour of the notion of international political economy (IPE), which for me is simply the analysis of the structures that underlie the world in which international organisations operate, for it is these which effectively shape outcomes.' (Cox, 1999b: 390). He began reading Gramsci, and returned to Giambattista Vico and Marx. The shift became apparent in his published work and was to culminate (during the next decade and a half) in the three publications (1981, 1983, 1987) that are representative of his core theoretical framework.

The article 'On Thinking about Future World Order' (1976) published in *World Politics*, serves as a first example of this shift. In fact, it reflects many of the ideas that would be further developed in the first *Millennium* (1981) article. It is essential, therefore, to discuss it in some detail. Cox starts by identifying three approaches to 'thinking about the future'; the natural-rational approach, the positivist-evolutionary approach, and the historicist-dialectical approach. In the rest of the article he illustrates and criticises the application of the first two, and motivates his preference for the historicist-dialectical approach.

Cox (1976: 177–8) views the natural-rational approach as assuming the universality of human nature. Furthermore, it proposes that the world can be understood in terms of the inner and the outer. The outward appearances of humans struggling to realise their potential are visible in their various forms (institutions and behaviour). Through reason (derived from the universality of human nature assumption) we may understand the 'real essence of man and the polity'. Corresponding to 'inner' and 'outer' are subjective and objective principles, respectively. The subjective principle resides in the capacity of humans to deal with the challenges in constructing and upholding 'the polity'. The objective principle is related to the external constraints (nature) which humans have to confront and overcome to attain their potential. Drawing on Machiavelli (and thereby showing consistency), Cox argues that objective circumstances may be 'understood and manipulated' when 'creative ability in politics' is strengthened by the will to overcome (*necessità*). In attempting to attain the ideal while having to deal with external constraints, polities will rise and decline (history is cyclical). During times when they possess 'creative energy' (*virtù*) they will rise, but in the absence thereof, 'civic spirit' is replaced by the 'pursuit of particular interests'. Cox views this approach as having 'critical potential', because it compares the ideal with the *status quo* and because of the acceptance that there is a link between the subjective and objective principles.

The positivist-evolutionary approach rejects the complementarity of the inward/outward approach to understanding. It is, 'Scientific method for the study of society...conceived as analogous to that evolved for the study of the world of nature'[3] (Cox, 1976: 178). Talcott Parsons' structural-functionalism is described by Cox as fitting within this approach, and is seen by him as standing in the service of 'problem-solving'. Why? Because it is used to explain and facilitate the end goal of industrial societies: maximum productivity and societal stability. Essentially, Cox equates here (for the first time) the positivist approach with problem-solving. No reference to Horkheimer's distinction between critical theory and traditional theory is made (see Chapter 4). To account for change, this approach (in terms of the 'systems' concept in structural-functionalism) uses the notion of 'systemic feedback'. Systemic dynamics (change) are explained in terms of outputs and modified inputs. He then criticises this view of 'change' because it projects current trends and outputs while assuming that the social relations and organisation upon which they rest will not change, 'The existing distributions of power…are considered as given…' Cox (1976: 180–1).

Turning to the historicist-dialectical approach, Cox's (1976: 181) first observation is that this approach accepts the notion of dualism (subjective/objective) as posed by the natural-rational perspective. However, it does not distinguish between, nor does it separate the subjective ideal and the 'objective conditions of existence'. It attempts to explain objective events by connecting them to the subjective 'idea', put differently and more to the point, 'The social world is intelligible as the creation of the human mind.' (Cox, 1976: 181). The historical method (or historicism) therefore attempts to understand 'historical process' in terms of how the subject engages with the outside world.[4] Secondly, this approach attempts to understand events (action and thought) by locating them within the 'larger totality'. It emphasises, therefore, the view of the complex whole in order to arrive at understanding. Thirdly, it tries to generalise by developing ideal types (for example, feudalism and capitalism) related to specific historical phases. These types are found within 'a coherent structural arrangement of ideas, behaviour patterns, and institutions' (Cox, 1976: 182).[5]

Fourth, the dialectical aspect of the approach is crucial in the explanation of change. Quoting Ralph Dahrendorf, Cox introduces what he would later call 'contradictions'. This is the idea that societies change because of the appearance of 'antagonisms' within them. These changes may come about because of an increasing gap between a prevalent idea of society (or a world view) and the real material conditions which people (or groups of people) experience. When these contradictions develop, the potential for conflict and/or change becomes latent. Whether conflict/change actually occurs depends on 'a change of consciousness on the part of the potential challengers and their adoption of a contrast image of society'. Reflecting his reading of Gramsci, Cox ends the discussion of the historicist-dialectical approach, by stressing the need for the 'historical-dialectical analyst' to not only analyse the world, but also to 'arouse consciousness and the will to act' (Cox, 1976: 182–3).

In the rest of the article, Cox considers the application of the natural-rational and positivist-evolutionary approaches to the issue of world order. He starts by looking at liberal pluralism as '…the political arrangement most conducive of the good life' and a normative base for world order'. In political practice, however, he argues that it was soon discovered that the assumption of the modernisation paradigm that accompanies liberal pluralism – economic development leads to democracy – did not hold up in the developing world. To account for this, the appearance of authoritarianism was explained as being a necessary 'function' of 'underdeveloped political structures'. The fact that it is extremely difficult to bring about the condition of political pluralism under conditions where power is very unevenly distributed was, however, ignored. Cox (again) cites Machiavelli's concept of *necessità*: '...the material conditions that must be taken into account in shaping action toward the normative goal, has been deficient' (Cox, 1976: 187).

Subsequently, he looks at theories that have their origin in the positivist-evolutionary approach, particularly those that he encountered and used during his time at the ILO. In this approach, world order is viewed as a problem that can be 'solved' through institutions (international organisations) that advance global integration. He singles out David Mitrany's functionalism, and the neo-Functionalism of Ernst Haas (citing Haas' *Beyond the Nation-State*, which he had earlier used as a model for his article on 'The Executive Head') to illustrate the point. With respect to Haas' approach to how international integration can be facilitated and analysed, Cox (1976: 189) concludes (and thereby leaving the 'positivist phase' behind): 'It had become largely a checklist of concepts drawn up in relation to the question as to whether the international system was becoming more centralized.'

He then moves on to discuss two other approaches to international integration in vogue at the time, transnationalism and transgovernmentalism. Cox (1976: 192) notes that they both make the same mistake; they perceive 'the future in terms of the magnification of one currently observable tendency'. For transnationalism the tendency (trend) was the rise of the multinational corporation (MNC) that would lead to the development of political arrangements that surpassed the state. For transgovernmentalism the trend of increasing transnationalism and economic interdependence would lead to the need for greater direct coordination and interaction between the bureaucracies of states, thereby enhancing the role of international organisations and decreasing the role of foreign affairs departments. Both approaches took these trends and projected them into the future, ignoring the fact that when trends become observable, they are often approaching the point when the process is reversed. Such projections take the parameters of the system as a constant, and do not envisage events, which may lead to 'a change of the system rather than merely changes within the system,' (Cox, 1976: 190, 196).

In contrast, the historicist-dialectical approach leads the analyst to focus on events such as a change in 'the balance of social forces within the state', as well as change 'in the nature of the state'. Citing the historian, Geoffrey Barraclough, Cox notes the importance of 'structural changes' such as population growth, industrialisation, and ideas and attitudes. The approach also incorporates the crucial issue of power; '...order refers, in the first instance, to the distribution and mechanism of power' (Cox, 1976: 192–3, 195). To account for change, therefore, requires a focus on (contradictions) within states, and on the distribution of power between social forces. These dynamics will also have an effect on the nature of the international system. Cox (1976: 196) concludes by drawing on Fernand Braudel's notion of the synchronic and diachronic dimensions of time. The former focuses on the here and now; how are societies linked to a specific world order? The latter focuses on the contradictions, the reshaping of power relations over a prolonged period of time.

The year of publication of the next article, 1977, coincides with Cox's acceptance of a position at York University in Toronto, Canada. Columbia was an intellectually inspiring and open environment, but his long absence from Canada and the nurtured intent to eventually return there, influenced his decision to relocate.[6] But there was also the contrast between what he experienced at Columbia and his expectations that were based on events (the late 1960s, when the campus was the site of radical protests and student agitation during the years preceding his move there). The students, he remarked during the interview with Germain (1999b: 391), who had been critical during the later 1960s '...were no longer revolutionary at all. They were much more concerned with getting on with their careers'.

Another reason which played a role in Cox's decision to return to Canada was the contrast he experienced between the '...ideological homogeneity of the business executive class' who lived in the Connecticut suburb of New York City (where he resided in order to be close to the university) and the 'cultural mix of Geneva's international milieu'. Therefore, although he was appreciative of the 'liberal intellectual environment of excellence' at Columbia, he looked forward to his position at a new university with a young and vibrant department; Toronto was also completely different from the parochial Anglo-Protestant place he remembered when he lived in Montreal. It had become a vibrant, cosmopolitan city 'with a view on the whole world' (Cox, 1996b: 30 and personal communication, 23 October 2007).

By this time, Cox was (re) reading Collingwood, Vico, Braudel and Gramsci. The Gramscian notion of hegemony is introduced in the 'Decision making' (with Harold Jacobson) and 'Labor and Hegemony' articles (both published in 1977). I will deal with the collaborative article first. This article stems from the volume (also with Jacobson) *The Anatomy of Influence* (1972), and is an attempt to cast the results of their research within a new framework that takes account of the importance of the context in which decisions are made. This context may be local, national or global, but during times of change the more specific focus on decision-making within institutions, requires the analyst to pull back in order to better understand the broader context. It requires a shift to the global context of power relations, and would need to sketch a 'structural picture of power relations', a focus on the possibilities for conflict and change, and the role of international organisations in perpetuating or transforming power relations (Cox and Jacobson, 1977: 350–1, 356).

Cox and Jacobson (1977: 357) identify three perspectives on power: state power, economic power and social power. Their conceptualisation of social power foreshadows the conceptualisation of power as it is used in Cox's core theoretical framework. State power, they argue, while an essential component of power relations in the world system, cannot be equated with a 'state-centric' view of power. The latter view, in effect, would limit the study of power in the global system to inter-state relations, and essentially the study of the power relations of the strong states that originated in Europe. At the second level (economic power), there is a view of power that also takes into account non-state aspects of the world system, '...economic relations, and the movements of people and ideas'. However, it does so from a perspective that focuses on how the state influences economics in response to societal demands (welfare). The state is, therefore, an important aspect within their conceptualisation of economic power (Cox and Jacobson, 1977: 357–8).

Social power (Cox and Jacobson's first choice) takes account of state power and non-state power. It is a model of power that originates in society, and is based on which social groups or classes (dominant and subordinate) have control over production. Because production is 'internationalised', the concept of social power can be extended to the use of control over production between social groups in different states. Such a view of power, they argue, can be state or non-state (as in the relationship between states and MNC's). State and non-state actors use social power. Therefore, the power relations of the world system have to be thought of as existing within '...the structure of international production relations'. This includes the impact of state policy on the economy, and via the economy on international production relations. They conclude that, '...production relations can be a common yardstick, to which the other levels of power can be reduced' (Cox and Jacobson, 1977: 358–9).[7]

In the next section of the article, Cox and Jacobson (1977: 359–61) outline a model of a world system configured around the structure of international production relations. It is interesting to note that, at this stage, the concept 'world system' is derived from Wallerstein (1976, 1979). A single system characterised by a hierarchy based on the division of labour (depending on what is produced and who controls it).[8] Thus, there are core states (the industrialised North), semi-peripheral states (newly industrialised states), and peripheral states (poor states, with 'limited development prospects'). Wallerstein's core-periphery model is subsequently used to identify another five categories of states. It is important, for our purposes, to take note of three of these classifications because they are regarded as potential sources of conflict in the world system.

Innovations in production, research and development are located in the 'postindustrial' core states. In these states, 'alienation' is identified as a potential source of conflict (contradiction), because of '...that large part of their population not engaged in the core economic activities' (Cox and Jacobson, 1977: 361). The states of 'dependent capitalism' are those states who have attained a degree of industrialisation and who import consumer goods from the core, and have managed to market themselves as export zones for the MNC's core states. Sources of conflict here are the possibility of protectionist trade policies, and the growing inequality between sectors of the population who are marginalised from, and those who are integrated into the industrial sector of the economy. Then there are the poor states, with hardly any development to look forward to. They are not essential for the functioning of the world economy (except in cases where they possess essential raw materials for core production), but may be a source of regional and global instability. Their problems are viewed by 'those more integrated into international production as problems of global poor relief and potentially of global riot control' (Cox and Jacobson, 1977: 361).

The conceptualisation of (hegemonic) power is derived from Gramsci. Power cannot depend on material capacity alone. The exercise of power depends on a combination of material aspects and ideas/ideology. The legitimacy that is accorded to the *status quo* is rooted in a dominant ideology. This ideology and the distribution of power determine what issues (problems) are focused on. The problems which are on the scientific agenda are usually related to factors which could threaten the continued existence of the system, as well as the power relations upon which it is based. Cox and Jacobson (1977: 363–4) introduce the concept of hegemony to refer to the way in which a dominant group in society exercises power. The latter cannot only rely on its control over the material components of power, it must also establish consensus (and thereby the incorporation) of subordinate groups. Consensus is achieved by ensuring that some benefits are distributed to the subordinate group, through '…a program that can be plausibly represented as of universal interest'.

Returning to the context within which international organisations make decisions, Cox and Jacobson (1977: 364) emphasise that (international) institutions reflect hegemony as well. They hereby make the controversial 'jump' from Gramsci's application of hegemony to the relations between dominant and subordinate groups in state-society relations, to the application of this concept at the international level. Accordingly, the formation of an international organisation reflects the contemporary 'hegemonic consensus' related to a specific international issue. The important question therefore, becomes whether the contemporary world order reflects a condition of hegemony, or not.

The explanation of change also requires a consideration of the nature of hegemony at the internalional level. The possibility of institutional change cannot be investigated without an analysis of the likelihood of hegemonic change at the international level. Such a change may occur when the material power capabilities of a subordinate group are increased, and when the subordinate group can muster a counter-hegemonic challenge to the prevalent ideology, meaning, 'a coherent and persistent articulation of...demands that challenge the legitimacy of the prevailing consensus' (Cox and Jacobson, 1977: 365). The first reaction by the dominant group will be to address a counter-hegemonic challenge by attempting to satisfy some demands without effecting any radical change of the system as a whole. This strategy amounts to further co-optation. In the absence of the possibility to achieve revolutionary change, the alternative is a compromise, which is arrived at through negotiations. The demands (by developing states, supported by the United Nations Conference on Trade and Development – UNCTAD) for a New International Economic Order (NIEO) is viewed as an example of a counter-hegemonic challenge.

The article concludes by identifying and considering some 'proximate factors' which could have an impact on power relations, and therefore also on the state of hegemony. First, there are those who influence foreign policy decisions in core states. Second, transnational interest groups such as MNC's and other non-governmental organisation's (NGO's) actors, as well as transgovernmental relations (relations between specialised state bureaucracies in international organisation forums). This is derived from Keohane and Nye (1974). The interests of private transnational groups tend to be 'economic-corporative' in nature (sourced from Gramsci). This means that they are primarily concerned with the particular interest of the group they represent. They will be supportive of a particular kind of hegemony, if their interests are accommodated. Those involved in transgovernmental relations are more directly concerned with the existing power relations that relate to hegemony.

Third, those who may be able to take the initiative as 'empathetic neutrals'. During a period, which is potentially conducive to hegemonic change, their role would be to act as mediators between hegemonic and counter-hegemonic forces, so as to arrive at a historical comprise. Heads of international organisations, prominent individuals, or the foreign policies of smaller states could play this role. Lastly, there is public opinion. Cox and Jacobson note that international organisations for all intents and purposes hardly have any interaction with 'mass constituencies'. The interests of the latter, if they are represented at all, are channeled through national bureaucracies and special interest groups. Nevertheless, they deem it 'useful' to investigate how much broad-based participation on global issues can have an impact on reshaping hegemony, and how much it can act as a political foundation to address these issues. This is an important point, and is related to Murphy's (2007) conclusion that critical theory in IR/IPE has not managed to produce research that empirically incorporates and focuses on 'mass constituencies' (Cox's, 1999a marginalised and precarious groups). Cox and Jacobson argue that an awareness of how global issues affect the welfare of the poor in developing states can only come about through the raising of consciousness and mobilisation. They conclude (optimistically), that broad-based participation in international organisations, though far off, should not be discounted (Cox and Jacobson, 1977: 367–70).

In the last three articles under review in this chapter, Cox returns to some of the above issues and introduces some new concepts. In 'Labor and Hegemony', he (1977) discusses the relationship between the ILO and the US, arguing that the US withdrew from the organisation because it perceived that the ILO was moving away from legitimating a specific form of production relations (tripartism). The historical method is used to analyse the dynamics between the ILO, the role of the executive head (director-general), the AFL-CIO (representing the interests of American labour), and the US government. Cox argues that changes in the international production structure and the accompanying change in social relations related to production, are linked to the corporative form of state. This form of state takes on different manifestations in the core industrialised and the developing (peripheral) states (Cox, 1977: 420–2).

Cox (1977: 421) reiterates his view on production as '...the ultimate resource on which political power rests'. He calls the type of production relations that the hegemonic coalition in the US (at the time) legitimated, 'tripartism'. This is one of the (twelve) modes of social relations of production that he later lists and discusses in PPWO (Cox, 1987). These modes are dealt with in greater detail in Chapter 3, and we need not elaborate here, except to say that the equivalent form in states that are in a position of 'dependent capitalism' is called 'state corporatism'. Cox (1977: 460), in an extended footnote (nr 7), cites Phillip Schmitter's (1974) work as being helpful in his own conceptualisation of corporatism. Nevertheless, he qualifies that Schmitter remains at the state level, while the way he uses the term is as a 'form of production relations'. A form that rests on the idea of class cooperation and in which participation and control takes place within state-based structures.

In a response to Douglas and Godson's (1980) critique of 'Labor and Hegemony', Cox (1980) makes some interesting observations on his own method and it is worth taking note of these, as we approach the next chapter. He identifies the perspective of Douglas and Godson (1980) as one, which is close to 'certain mainstream political science'. What implications does this have? It leads them to look at actors, the motives for their actions, and events that are the result of the interaction between them. Cox acknowledges that this is part of the process of enquiry, but that it leaves the analyst with an incomplete picture. What is required is an approach that accepts that action is given meaning by the context in which it takes place.

The essential first step is, therefore, to establish the context or 'historical structure' (this concept is sourced from Braudel, see also Cox, 1996b: 29 and Cox, 1986: 245–6) that forms the backdrop for action and which consists of (objective) power relations and (subjective) 'shared meanings'. Thereafter, must come '...the attempt to reconstruct the mental frameworks through which individuals and groups perceive their field of action'. Finally, the analyst must ask whether properly contextualised actions are potentially transformative or supportive of a historical structure. This requires a focus on the consequences, and not the motivation that results in the action (Cox, 1980: 474–5).

The last article I will look at is important for two reasons. First, because in it, Cox (1979: 416, footnote 1) sets out his own values or 'political position'. Secondly, because here Cox explains in some detail his view on ideology and science. Put differently, in the article he sets out his perception of epistemology. His purpose is to show how ideology, politics and knowledge are linked and how this can be seen in various 'clusters' of research networks surrounding a particular issue. The issue he investigates is the literature surrounding the demands for a NIEO at the UN during the 1970s. More specifically, he identifies (through a survey of the literature) various perspectives (monopolistic liberalism, social democratic, Third World, neo-Mercantilist, and historical materialism) and discusses the 'research networks' connected to them in some detail.

From the outset, Cox states his position on the 'scientific' status of approaches in the social sciences, particularly those 'establishment' perspectives that reveal (once one removes their appeal to universality) an argument that, though it is historically fleeting, puts the case for contemporary well-established interests. This statement is the forerunner of the much quoted 'theory is always for someone and for some purpose' premise of the 1981 *Millennium* article (see Chapter 3). Cox confirms Neufeld's (see Chapter 4) reading of his view on perspectives (incommensurable but comparable), when he points out that they can be (and are chosen) on the grounds of one's own value preferences.

In Cox's (1979: 376–7) case these are reflected in the following excerpts which are worth quoting in full: 'It is...only fair to warn the reader that my purpose in undertaking this survey was to discover and encourage avenues of enquiry that might in the long run aid towards the transformation of power relations both within and among nations in the direction of greater social equity' and therefore, '...I found the work of some of the radical neomercantilists and historical materialists discussed below more potentially valuable... than the more prestigious products of the western academic establishments'.

With respect to the establishment perspective, he concludes that attempts to deal with the demands for a NIEO reflect co-optation strategies. This translates into a research focus on what adjustments can be made to ensure wider acceptability (consensus/legitimacy) of the existing order, without making any major changes to the norms and regulations on which it is based. Furthermore, the use of (social) science goes through two stages. It is initially accepted as 'valid' as long as it serves as an aid to action during a particular time period, and it becomes ideology when its concepts and ideas are used to validate a particular order. Over time, any 'new science...will be perceived as ideology tied to historical foundations that have in turn become obsolete' (Cox, 1979: 415–16).

Finally, a number of other points made in the article are noteworthy. Cox (1979: 410) introduces the concept 'state class' which he sources from Elsenhans. The idea of a state class refers to the privileged elite in developing states who must be pressurised from below to ensure that they remain committed to 'national development goals'. This pressure should come from the disadvantaged, or from the latter in alliance with disaffected members of the state class. An important prerequisite is that marginalised groups must be receptive to being mobilised in order for them to exert any form of pressure. This condition is normally present in developing states immediately after decolonisation.

Cox (1979: 414) also hints at his impending critique of Wallerstein that would be stated in more unequivocal terms later. At this stage, he questions the notion that there is a single mode of production at the world system level and stresses the need to define the term. He regards this as a major shortcoming in the historical materialist perspective (specifically, world systems theory), which sets out to base its explanation on the concept of production; 'Theorizing about the world system has achieved a certain academic status, but relatively little is being done towards a better understanding of the varieties of the real world of production'.

What, to sum up, does the analysis of some of Cox's important pre-1987 publications point to? The development of CCT, originated during Cox's time at the ILO. This can be attributed to his realisation that its ideas on labour relations were relevant for a minority of the world's workers (those in the industrial sector). Although the ILO tried to engage with other (more marginalised) workers, it did so from within its own institutional structure (based on tripartism) which resulted in the exclusion of the overwhelming majority of workers. Also, his thoughts were shaped and influenced from various sources. The notion of the interactive, mutual influence between production processes, the nature (form) of the state, and changes at the international level were taken from the work of E.H. Carr. From George Sorel, Cox absorbed the understanding of historical materialism as consisting of a link between ideas and material conditions, as well as his skepticism towards positivism.

People have shared understandings of the social practices and institutions that they create to deal with material challenges. Change must, therefore, be understood in terms of changes in (intersubjective) thought and its link to materialist conditions. The notion of 'rethinking the thought of the past' is sourced from the historian, R.G. Collingwood in conjunction with Sorel. Crucially, for Cox, ideas always evolve within a particular historical context and it is essential to ask where a particular idea came from, and in whose interest the institutionalisation of such an idea is/was.

Cox's earlier work, was more inclined towards the positivist method, although he always emphasised the need to historically contexualise. During his last years at the ILO, Cox (together with Jeffrey Harrod) completed a major research project on different types of production relations and began to conceptualise and apply Gramsci's notion of hegemony to the explanation of the role of international organisations. This change in thinking was influenced by the current affairs of his time and by what he saw as the increasing gap between ideology and reality.

After his resignation from the ILO, and the move to academia he began to conceptualise and set out the assumptions of his core theoretical framework, drawing on a variety of sources, but starting out with Gramsci and a re-reading of Marx and Giambattista Vico. On epistemology and method we have noted that the critical potential of an approach lies in its willingness to ask whether practice reflects the normative goal/ideal of the polity. Thoughts and events are connected in explanation; one cannot separate the two as positivism does (here Cox draws on Machiavelli, Collingwood and Vico). The positivist approach to the creation of knowledge is a 'problem-solving' one. Its explanations are coupled to system maintenance and systemic efficiency.

As an alternative to positivism, Cox proposes the historical-dialectical approach (Cox draws on Vico to support his argument, see endnote 3 of this chapter) that accepts the link between ideas and events (sourced from Collingwood). The main strengths of this approach, Cox argues, are that it is holistic, it attempts to develop generalisations related to ideal types, it explains change in terms of contradictions arising in society and that it adopts a 'contrast image of society' by would be challengers (sourced from Gramsci). It also stresses the importance of analysing the material conditions, and the effect of structural changes on forms of state and the 'balance of social forces within the state' (sourced from Barraclough). Lastly, it uses two dimensions of time, synchronic and diachronic (sourced from Braudel). From Braudel too, comes the notion that the analyst needs to establish the historical structure within which the consequences of actions take place.

The 'whole' within which events take place needs to be understood in terms of the condition of hegemony. Hegemony (or the absence thereof) is the context within which the potential for change needs to be understood. Furthermore, hegemony requires us to think of power in terms of material capacity and ideology. Hegemony is based on coercion and consensus. Contradictions (possibly leading to conflict) in the world system can be seen in terms of the alienation of social forces related to production in the core states, and marginalisation in the semi-periphery and periphery. Hegemony may be analysed in terms of state-society relations, but it may also be prevalent at the international level. For instance, when international organisations reflect a contemporary hegemonic idea.

From this we can derive the following premises:

- Contradictions (a gap between the prevalent ideology and material conditions) can lead to change/conflict.
- The potential for change/conflict depends on a 'change of inter-subjective understanding' and the adoption of a 'contrast image of society' by would be challengers.
- Changes in power relations between groups within society, have an influence on the form of state.
- Changes in state form are related to changes in the international system.
- Transformation or change can be explained by investigating whether hegemony is prevalent.

The possibility of popular participation in international organisations is reflected in Cox's later (post-1987) work on multilateralism, while the role of the foreign policies of smaller states in challenging hegemony is returned to in 'middlepowermanship' (Cox, 1989a). Important and related to the future potential of CCT is the question that arose from the discussion of the role and potential of broad-based opinion: 'The poor of the world, as a whole, remain very largely inarticulate' (Cox and Jacobson, 1977: 369). But to what extent has this changed? How do contemporary marginalised social forces engage with their material and ideational environment?

3
The Core Theoretical Framework and Beyond

This chapter focuses on Cox's core theoretical framework as it is set out in the two *Millennium* articles (1981, 1983) and in *Production, Power, and World Order: Social Forces in the Making of History* (1987). It also touches on Cox's post-1987 thinking about aspects such as the changing world order (globalisation and the nature of the state), multilateralism, and civilisations. Cox's modes of social relations of production typologies are discussed and related to his identification of three contemporary social hierarchies, the marginalised, precarious and integrated. I also point to the continuing relevance of the core theoretical framework for the analysis of the contemporary world order. Lastly, the chapter engages with the challenging requirement of the historic method to access the 'collective images' of subordinated groups (the marginalised).

Engaging with Waltzian neo-Realism

In light of the fact that CCT and three of the four authors (see Chapter 5) associated with a critical theory of IR (Ashley, Linklater and Hoffman), set out their arguments in opposition to Waltz's (1979) *Theory of International Politics*, this section provides a brief overview of Waltz's book. Arguably, Waltzian neo-Realism was one of the major issues that dominated the 'inter-paradigm' debate during the 1980s (Griffiths, 1999: 47). The reactions were mixed, but the critics were vociferous in their condemnation of an argument that they believed was *status quo* orientated (supportive of bipolarity and superpower politics). The debate led to the publication of an edited volume by Robert Keohane in 1986, *Neorealism and its Critics*.

Waltz starts by setting out the criteria and assumptions that underpin the deductive-nomological model of explanation, which is prevalent in the natural sciences, but more contested in the social sciences. He regards it as a superior approach to 'the problem of explanation' and much more likely to lead to the ability to predict and control then the inductive approach to the development of theory. His understanding of theory '...does not accord with usage in much of traditional political theory, which is concerned more with philosophic interpretation than with theoretical explanation', but relates more to how it is used and understood in the natural sciences and also in certain disciplines in the humanities (for example, Economics) (Waltz, 1979: 6). In this sense, Waltz sets up his explanatory theory of international politics (based on the systemic principles of the balance of power and the absence of central authority) as 'scientifically defensible' (Griffiths, 1999: 47).

In contrast to the prevalent 'interdependence' approach of the 1970s (Keohane and Nye, 1971; Keohane and Nye, 1974; Keohane and Nye, 1977 and Morse, 1976) Waltz emphasises the importance of focusing on the utilitarian ('self-help') state, functioning within the dynamics of an anarchic system. This is an essential point of departure for the construction of a good theory of international politics. Before setting out the principles of his 'systemic' or 'structuralist' explanation of state behaviour, however, Waltz (1979: 18, 38) turns his attention to two types of theory in the literature of international politics, 'reductionist theories' and 'systemic approaches and theories'.

In the chapter on reductionist theories he examines and criticises Lenin and Hobson's economic imperialism theories and Galtung's structural theory of imperialism. These are found wanting because they attempt to link a systemic phenomenon, war, to the economic attributes (capitalism) of the stronger states (or similarly, but in Wallersteinian terms, the attributes of the 'core' states). To this argument Waltz (1979: 36) responds that many different types of states have, at some stage, followed imperialist policies, 'Yet the theories we have examined claim that an imperial relation exists because the imperial state has certain economic attributes.' Waltz's point is that one cannot explain the functioning of any system by focusing on the attributes of the units, which are the component parts of that system.

Next, Waltz examines some theories that, at the time of his writing, claimed to offer a systemic explanation to the study of international politics. How does Waltz understand systemic explanation? When, systemic attributes are present '...one cannot predict outcomes or understand them merely by knowing the characteristics, purposes, and interactions of the system's units' (Waltz, 1979: 39). The behaviour of the component units (states) must be explained by an organising principle that lies at the systems level. Waltz goes on to review two systemic explanations by Richard Rosecrance and Stanley Hoffmann and finds them inadequate because 'For Hoffmann, and especially for Rosecrance, the important explanations are found at the level of states and of statesmen; the systems level thus becomes all product and is not at all productive' (Waltz, 1979: 50).

Although the claims that are made by Morton Kaplan's systems approach are 'bold enough to leave one breathless', Waltz (1979: 50, 56) concludes that his attempt at the development of a systems theory fails because of his inability to differentiate between unit interaction and systemic attributes. Waltz (1979: 53–4) offers two specific reasons for this conclusion. First, systemic changes (or 'disturbances') in Kaplan's model are brought about by the actions of states (the component units) that do not abide by systemic rules. There is, therefore, no outside 'environment' that feeds into the international system. Kaplan regards states as being a part of the environment. Second, states are conceptualised as 'subsystems' within the international system. The latter can even take on a 'subsystem dominant' shape, according to Kaplan. To this Waltz (1979: 54) responds, 'The mind boggles at the thought of subsystems being dominant, let alone sharing dominance. What could subsystems' dominance be other than the negation of a systems approach?'

Waltz's (1979: 63) alternative to these 'inside-out' explanations is to be found in his conceptualisation of the international political structure. The first systemic-level characteristic of this structure is 'The enduring anarchic character of international politics [which] accounts for the striking sameness in the quality of international life through the millennia...' (Waltz, 1979: 66). This structural attribute (absence of central authority) affects the actions of states indirectly 'through socialization...and through competition among them' very much in the same way that the structural principles of markets influence individual entrepreneurs (Waltz, 1979: 74–6). The fact that all states have to assure their continued existence (their sovereignty) in a system with no central authority makes them alike. They are functionally undifferentiated (Waltz, 1979: 93, 97).

States differ, however, in their capabilities to perform this primary function effectively. This is Waltz's second structural attribute which, together with the first, determines how states are located relative to one another in the international system. Waltz (1979: 97–8) realises that he may be accused of falling into the same 'inside-out' explanation trap that he accuses others of, so the key terminology he insists on is 'distribution of capabilities' which is not an attribute of a unit (state) but a systemic concept. Together, the systemic attributes of anarchy and differential distribution of capabilities explain and predict the behaviour of states. This behaviour includes the formation of alliances, balancing strategies and the practice of 'balance of power politics' (Waltz, 1979: 128).

In the last two chapters of *Theory of International Politics*, Waltz argues that a concentrated distribution of capabilities among fewer states is preferable to a more even distribution (multipolarity) and concludes that a bipolar order (such as the one between the former Soviet Union and the United States during the Cold War) is better for system stability. I now return to the main focus of this chapter.

Problem-solving and critical theory

The development of Cox's thinking that has been traced thus far is brought together in the *Millennium* articles (1981 and 1983) and PPWO (1987). In addition to the assumptions, concepts and dynamics of his explanatory framework, Cox also provides us with a more nuanced motivation for his focus on production and his perspective on epistemology. He also singles out and criticises neo-Realism, world systems theory and Marxism. Although I regard these three publications as the nucleus of Cox's thinking on the method of historicism, where necessary, and to further clarify his concepts, ontology and epistemology, I also draw on his pre- and post-1987 publications.

The basic question that the core theoretical framework addresses is how are social forces (related to production) linked to forms of state, and to world orders?[1] To answer this question, Cox (1981: 86) argues, we need to move beyond the study of state and society as separate entities (as in neo-Realism). The distinction is, today, analytical, but in practice they have become so 'interpenetrated' that a more useful term is 'state-society complex'. The focus must be on the latter and how state-society complexes are related to different forms of states. This approach, while being somewhat on the margins of mainstream IR, can be discerned in the work of E.H. Carr, Eric Hobsbawm and Fernand Braudel.

Although Wallersteins' world systems theory draws on Braudel, Cox (1981: 86–7) notes that it underplays the impact that states can have on the world system (in Coxian terms, world order). Wallerstein views states as being mainly the captives of their position within a single world (capitalist) system. Secondly, world systems theory has the 'unintended' consequence of focusing on aspects that maintain the system. Instead, the analyst should be looking for contradictions, which could act as potential catalysts for systemic transformation.

I turn, next, to a more detailed analysis of Cox's view on epistemology, his method of historicism, and how this is related to his critique of neo-Realism and (progressive and scientific) Marxism. Cox's (1981: 87) position on theory accepts that knowledge is connected to interests, 'Theory is always *for* someone and *for* some purpose' and that 'There is...no such thing as theory in itself, divorced from a standpoint in time and space'. This leads him to make the distinction between 'critical theory' and 'problem-solving theory.' It is a distinction that has often been used by readers of Cox to incorrectly link him to the CT of the Frankfurt School (via Max Horkheimer's distinction between 'critical theory' and 'traditional theory', see Chapter 4).

What does Cox regard as the defining characteristics of problem-solving theory? The first point to take note of is that it is *status quo* oriented. It deals with issues that arise from within the parameters of the dominant power dynamics and the institutions within which they are located and play themselves out. The purpose is to ensure that these relations and institutions operate efficiently (again, this reflects Cox's own experience at the ILO). In this sense problem-solving theory is 'ahistorical', because it views the contemporary parameters of the system (for instance, state power politics) as being a mirror of the past and of the future (Cox views Waltzian neo-Realism in this light). This assumption (of a universal fixed order) is not only related to method but, Cox argues, contains within it a normative bias itself. The bias is towards the interests of those who want a particular order to be maintained. The claim of value freedom by problem-solving (positivist) theory is, therefore, suspect (Cox, 1981: 88–9).

Critical theory (CCT), on the other hand, does not focus on problems by isolating them from the broader context, or by 'further analytical subdivisions' (Cox, 1981: 89–90). It also starts by looking at an aspect of social action, but then pulls away to locate such activity within the context of the whole system. It does not deal with problems by attempting to resolve them so that the system functions more efficiently, but asks how the system gave rise to the problems in the first instance. Drawing away from the current order, it asks what the origin of that order is and how it developed. Problem-solving and critical theory, are both connected to practice. The former as a guide to 'tactical action' in order to maintain the *status quo*, the latter as a guide to 'strategic action' aimed at changing it. The method of historicism forms a crucial part of CCT, and this will be returned to in more detail below. At this stage, we can note that Cox (1981: 89) regards critical theory as a '...theory of history'. However, it does not only look at past actions, but also at history as an ongoing process characterised by change.

It is important to point out that Cox does not refer to standing 'apart from the prevailing order' (pulling away) to indicate that it is possible to separate subject and object. His normative preference for an alternative order based on social equity is never denied, nor does he deny his own subjectivity: '...I accept that my own thought is grounded in a particular perspective; and I mean no offense in pointing to what appears to be a similar grounding in other people's thought' (Cox, 1986: 247). The idea encapsulated in 'standing apart from' is related to the holistic component of Cox's critical theory and to the need to think of the possibility of an alternative order.

Nevertheless, the contemplation of an alternative order must be anchored in a (realistic) understanding of history. Strategies, which are considered for practical action, must be based on '...changing practice and empirical-historical study, which are a proving ground for concepts and hypotheses.' Thus, we need to consider the possibility of an alternative order in a non-utopian manner; critical theory '...must reject improbable alternatives just as it rejects the permanency of the existing order' (Cox, 1981: 87, 90).[2]

Historicism: The essence of CCT

One way of approaching the topic of the historical method in CCT, is by locating it in Cox's criticism of Waltz's neo-Realism (1979) (see above) and his discussion of Marx.

Cox (1981: 91) does not view classical realism as being incompatible with his view of critical theory. The realism of E.H. Carr and Ludwig Dehio are rooted in a 'historical mode of thought' because, they historically demarcated the make up of actors related to specific international systems and attempted to understand accompanying institutions, explanations and actions within the context of the time they appear in. However, he blames Morgenthau (1948, 1951) and Waltz (1979) for turning classical realism into problem-solving theory. This must be understood and explained within the context of the Cold War and the resultant foreign policy focus in the US on power expansion and management. This (American) version of realism is a 'science at the service of big-power management of the international system' (Cox, 1986: 248).

Neo-Realism assumes that there is a 'common rationality' with which the international system may be understood. This rationality is informed by three premises: first, that human nature is unchanging and is informed by a selfish disposition to maximise power; second, that the foreign policies of states are alike – they are informed by the need to ensure political security in the national interest; and third, that the international system acts as a constraint on power maximising states through the balance of power mechanism (Cox, 1981: 92). These premises, moreover, are unchanging and universal. History, as viewed by neo-Realism, is continuity. The events, which play themselves out over time, are merely illustrations of variations, which are informed by the same three underlying premises. In the words of Waltz, it is a science that claims to 'transcend history' and therefore the 'future will always be like the past' (Waltz, responding to a question at the American Political Science Association in 1980) (Cox, 1981: 117, footnote 6).

In contrast, CCT is informed by the method of historicism and neo-Realism is informed by the method of positivism. The positivist method, according to Waltz, enables the analyst to separate from that which is to be known – the 'externally perceived events.' These events consist of actors (states) who are responsible for causing a change in the behaviour of other actors (states) in a system, which operates according to the principle (law) of the balance of power. Cox (1981: 93), however, argues that the claim of value freedom is transparent. While neo-Realism predicts that states will behave according to the premises of its theory, it also contributes, in practice, to convert policy-makers to its perspective of rationality. The advice to act in accordance with the dictates of the approach is essential to ensure that the 'actors' in effect perceive the inter-state system in this way.

The method of historicism, on the other hand, asserts that there is a unity of subject and object. Cox (1981: 93–4) sources this premise from Vico (originally 1774, translated version by Bergin and Fisch, 1970). In a revealing statement, he asserts that for him, 'The Vichian approach... is that of critical theory'. This point is an important one, bearing in mind the supposed link with the Frankfurt School of CT (Chapter 4) and the categorisation of Cox as a neo-Gramscian (see below). Both are incorrect. If one had to partake in the practice of 'guilt through association', a more accurate description of CCT would be neo-Vichian.

The assumption of unity between consciousness and being (Cox also uses E.P. Thompson as a source, Cox, 1996b: 27) is crucial to the explanation of change in the historical mode of understanding. History is perceived as the arena of change through the changing (not the 'unchanging' as in neo-Realism) nature of the human mind and the institutions that are collectively created by them. For Vico, '...the nature of man and of human institutions (among which must be included the state and the inter-state system) should not be thought of in terms of unchanging substance but rather as a continuing creation of new forms' (Cox, 1981: 93). Historicism, as used by Cox (via Vico's conceptualisation) is an approach in which institutions are viewed as 'collective responses to a collectively perceived problematic that produce certain practices' (Cox, 1986: 242).

Related to the genealogy of CCT, it is interesting to note that Cox refers to the fourteenth century Islamic historian, Ibn Khaldun, to illustrate how a similar kind of thinking on change and transformation can develop across time and within different civilisations. Khaldun was concerned with understanding what lay behind the 'events-history' of his own time – a period which was characterised by the decline of Islamic influence and North African civilisation. It was his purpose to understand what was responsible for the transformation he was experiencing. What was the 'internal logic' that was driving it? (Pasha, 1997: 5–58, 68 and Cox, 1992b: 152).

Cox's method of historicism and the materialist base upon which it rests owes (through Vico) much to Khaldun's 'science of culture.' Writing on the relevancy of Khaldun, Cox (1992b: 152) points to the importance of 'umran' (culture) in his thinking: '...the ways in which human communities confronted their specific problems of material existence'. According to Khaldun, 'rationally knowable principles' which explain historical change, revolve around the premise that humans organise collectively to confront the challenges of material existence. Through the creation of wealth beyond basic means of survival, greater needs are fulfilled such as social cohesion and reproduction. The state is the result of this co-operative endeavour and changes in accordance with the 'human intentionality' upon which it is based. It is not a fixed, ahistorical entity (Pasha, 1997: 60–2 and Cox, 1992b: 148).

But how are we to understand change? Change can be understood by accepting the unity between subject (the human mind) and object (institutions and practices). The latter are the result of collective responses to the challenges of the material (natural) environment (see also Cox, 1976), and we can therefore explain change through an understanding of the shared (intersubjective) ideas which people have of their institutions and practices. Institutions and practices do not exist in the same way as subjects do, but people respond and behave accordingly, because they (intersubjectively) share the same perception of these objective realities.

In the sense that people respond to their material environment historicism is the same as historical materialism, but the crux of CCT's historical method is to be found in the assertion that there is a link between the materialist world and ideas. The crucial task for the analyst is, therefore, '...To find the connections between the mental schema through which people conceive action and the material world which constrains both what people can do and how they can think about doing it' (Cox, 1986: 242–3). When asked to elaborate on the research program of historicism Cox (in the

'Postscript 1985'), responded that it is to explain the 'historical structures' related to particular periods and to point to the 'regularities' of human action in them. But, most importantly, it would have to focus on explaining how and why these structures change over time.

The method of historicism and the research focus of CCT is not aimed at coming up with law like generalisations or 'essences' related to human nature. Humans and the results of how they engage with their material world change gradually (Cox, 1986: 243–4). History is not the 'record' of universal truths; it reflects the dynamics of the different manifestations between the human mind and institutions. The 'conceit of scholars', according to Vico is to assume that their knowledge is universal, to take '…a form of thought derived from a particular phase of history (and thus from a particular structure of social relations) and assuming it to be universally valid' (Cox, 1981: 94). Herein we find another important assumption of CCT. But, after having noted the essence of the historical method, the question arises as to how the analyst must access the subjective frameworks which people use to determine a course of action in any particular historical structure. Are we to access them through '…an examination of the thought of the most perceptive minds of a period' as suggested by Cox? (1976: 182). If we did, we would be following Collingwood's premise that we need to rethink the thought of the past via individual subjectivity.

Linked to the challenge of 'inserting one's mind into the mentality' of people experiencing interaction with their material environment, are two (it seems) contradictory footnotes in the 1981 article and the 1985 'Postscript.' Also related is Cox's distinction between consequences of actions (which he regards as more important) and the individual motivation for them. In the *Millennium* article, when conceptualising the notion of 'collective images', Cox (1981: 99 and footnote 19 on page 119) emphasises that these are not compilations of individual attitudes, typically associated with the survey research method. Instead, 'they are coherent mental types'. In the 'Postscript' footnote, Cox (1986: 254, nr. 33) observes that explanation is the purpose of the historicism method and this requires '…an assembling of individual motivations and social structures to be connected by explanatory hypotheses.' Should this be interpreted as a contradiction? My interpretation is that it is not, because Cox does not reject positivism in toto: 'Regularities in human activities may indeed be observed...and thus the positivist approach can be fruitful within defined historical limits' (Cox, 1986: 244).

Historical materialism of a 'Special Kind'

In agreement with Vico, Cox (1981: 95) regards historical materialism as a '...foremost source of critical theory.' He emphasises, however, that he draws on the historical Marx, and not the structural Marxism of Althusser and Poulantzas. The latter he regards as similar to the method (not the assumptions) of neo-Realism, in the sense that it is maintained that the development of capitalism can be explained in accordance with unchanging, ahistorical laws. The historical Marx, however, views the mode of production and the class struggle as social phenomena, which can be explained by using 'historical reason.' What then, does Cox use from the historical Marx?

First, the concept 'dialectic'. Cox (1981: 95) explains his use of the term as being related to two levels: 'logic' and 'real history'. At the first level, dialectical thought requires that we focus on contradictions as a guide to explanation. Concepts, therefore, have to be held up against reality and must be adjusted to correspond to changing reality. Additionally, statements about reality contain their opposites within them. Both are aspects of a constantly changing truth. At the historical level, dialectic leads us to consider the possibility of alternatives. These alternatives emanate from 'opposed social forces in any concrete historical situation'. While neo-Realism focuses on conflict, its premise is that conflict recurs within an unchanging structure. The dialectical view of conflict, however, is that it may contribute to structural change. Secondly, the historical materialist approach incorporates a vertical dimension of relations. This means that we need to focus on power relations, not only, between powerful states, but also on a hierarchy that is based on the division of labour (core-periphery) (Cox, 1981: 95–6).

Thirdly, historical materialism 'opens up' the state, by focusing on the relations between state and civil society in a Gramscian sense. This means that the state is not regarded to be autonomous from civil society (as in neo-Realism). The relations between state and civil society are regarded as reciprocal, and subsequently, the state (as in economist determinist Marxism) is not merely an entity, which functions at the behest and in the general interest of capitalism. The interaction between the economic base and the 'ethico-political sphere' is one, which reflects interpenetration and mutual influence. Lastly, historical materialism leads us to focus on '…the production process as a critical element in the explanation of the particular historical form taken by a state/society complex.' Production generates material capabilities upon which the power of the state is based. Control over production, and the resultant power relations between social forces related to production are therefore of direct interest to the state and influence the form it takes (Cox, 1981: 96).

At this point, we need to expand more on the materialist aspect of Cox's method of historicism (see also Cox and Jacobson, 1977 and Cox, 1982). This materialist point of departure is (re)stated from the outset in PPWO: 'Production creates the material basis for all forms of social existence, and the ways in which human efforts are combined in productive processes affect all other aspects of social life, including the polity.' Cox (2002: 31), in reflection on this sentence, considers the first part of it to be pedestrian, because most of our existence (even thought) has a material foundation. Production, therefore, should be thought of as a 'process' and not in terms of 'existing things, i.e. products.'

The relationship between production and the political (power) is not 'unidirectional.' Power, as exercised by the state, also shapes and influences the dynamics of production. Moreover, production does not necessarily precede the state, historically (although it does have a 'certain logical precedence' in that it provides the material underpinnings of the state). The state has often shaped and guided forms of production (for example, the state's role in England to facilitate industrialisation and the transition to an unregulated economy during the nineteenth century). In any society, one type (form or mode) of production will be pre-dominant and this creates a hierarchy in terms of which wealth flows from the subordinate to the dominant classes (Cox, 1987: 1–5).

Is CCT guilty of material reductionism? In the sense that Cox views 'the production of the material basis of life as a fundamental activity for all human groups,' it can be so construed (Sinclair, 1996:

9). However, this is not the same as the economism of scientific Marxism, because Cox uses the Gramscian notion of the interpenetration between state and civil society. The state is not just the instrument of the dominant class, as it comes to '...embody certain general principles bearing on the regulations of production that act as a constraint on class interests narrowly conceived' (Cox, 1987: 19).

Additionally, while production involves work in order to directly satisfy human needs, it also creates the 'symbols and social institutions that make possible the cooperation among people required to do the first' (Cox, 1987: 13). Production, therefore, does not just refer to the economic activities of any society, it also includes the creation of the ideas, institutions and social practices which form the framework within which material production takes place; 'Looking at production is simply a way of thinking about collective life...' (Sinclair, 1996: 9, see also Cox, 1989b: 39 and Cox, 2002: 31).

On the relationship between power, production and the state, Cox (1987: 399–400) makes an important observation in the concluding section of PPWO: 'Although production was the point of departure of this study...the crucial role, it turns out, is played by the state. States create the conditions in which particular modes of social relations achieve dominance over coexisting modes, and they structure either purposively or by inadvertence the dominant-subordinate linkages of the accumulation process.' This comment confirms Cox's view of the state as being an important autonomous actor, albeit one whose actions are constrained by internal (the social forces or historic bloc which underpin it) and external factors (the dynamics of the global political economy). This is not a state whose actions and reason for existence can be singularly explained in terms of the material (production and accumulation) base of society.

Types (or modes) of production relations form the basis for the formation of classes. Cox (1987: 2–4) views the concept of class as providing us with the link between economics and politics (production and power). He emphasises, however, that we cannot apply this concept ahistorically. The concept cannot be transported from its origin in nineteenth century Europe and uncritically applied to contemporary production relations. Therefore, although production relations are the starting point for class formation '...other factors enter into the formation or nonformation of real historical classes', and the existence of class awareness must therefore be historically determined (Cox, 1987: 2).

Cox regards his initial research on labour relations as having facilitated a point of departure ('angle of vision') with which to look at the world, but not as a means to reduce the explanation of society and change to production and the role of labour. Essentially, the concept class refers to relations of domination and subordination. These relations can be found in a number of identities (gender, race, ethnicity, and religion) that can, in turn, be linked to production relations (Cox, 2002: 30). Classes, according to Cox (1987: 356), only exist when their propensity for joint action in addressing a social, political, economic problem has been demonstrated. Such a propensity may be discerned via the consequences of a joint action or the absence thereof (Cox, 1987: 407, footnote 8).

The dynamics of historical structures

Having set out the basic assumptions and premises (in terms of epistemology and method) of what he regards as critical theory, Cox moves on to dynamics. The framework within which 'action' takes place is the historical structure. Any historical structure consists of 'a particular configuration of forces.' These forces determine the dynamics within any given historical structure, and set the parameters within which social forces must act. They are material capabilities, ideas, and institutions which can be seen as the three points of a triangle which are connected by lines denoting mutual influence, 'No one-way determinism need be assumed among these three...' (Cox, 1981: 98). It is important to note that Cox is not a 'structuralist' in the sense that he views structure as the ultimate determinant of human action (as in the work of Levi-Strauss and Althusser). Structures are the result of 'collective human activities', and while they influence and constrain human action, they can be transformed by human action (Cox, 1987: 4).[3]

Material capabilities can be 'destructive' (military capacity) and 'productive.' Both are determined by, and are the result of technology, industry, organisational capacity, and wealth. *Ideas* are divided into 'intersubjective meanings' and 'collective images of social order'. Cox draws on Charles Taylor for his conceptualisation of intersubjective meaning. The concept refers to the shared perception that people have of institutions or practices. Their behaviour is determined by their shared understanding of an abstract idea. For example, the practice of negotiation or the institution of the state. Intersubjective meanings can be maintained over a prolonged period, but are also 'historically conditioned' and can change. Collective images which people have as groups (on the legitimacy of power relations, for instance), unlike intersubjective ideas, may differ and stand in opposition to one another. They can form the basis for the emergence of 'an alternative structure' (Cox, 1981: 99).

Lastly, we find (in any historical structure) *institutions*. They function to maintain, and are usually a mirror of, the prevailing power relations. Institutions can be hegemonic or non-hegemonic (see Cox and Jacobson, 1977). Hegemonic institutions accommodate diversity through consensus; which is grounded within a universal collective image (legitimacy) and distributes rewards to subordinate groups without endangering the position of the dominant group. In this way, legitimacy is ensured. Non-hegemonic structures are characterised by the use of power in a coercive manner and the absence (in varying degrees) of consensus (legitimacy). The existence of hegemony, however, depends not only on institutions but also on material capabilities and ideas/ideology (Cox, 1981: 99–100).

Cox (1983: 137–8) regards international organisations as institutions that can serve to maintain hegemony. This, again, is related to his own experience at the ILO (see Cox and Jacobson, 1977 and Cox, 1977). Essentially, they encapsulate and give voice to the 'universal norms' that are a part of the 'common-sense' ideology (for instance, a liberal world economy) of a hegemonic world order. Their function is, therefore, to uphold the rules that underpin the idea of a liberal world economy (the Bretton Woods institutions). They also act to incorporate the elites of subordinate states and, engage with ideas that challenge the hegemonic order. Decision-making processes are weighted in favour of states and social forces who support the hegemonic order. These institutions and their rules are created/shaped by the state (in alliance with other states), for whose benefit the hegemonic order exists. As such, they mirror perspectives that favour dominant state and economic classes.

Challenges by elites from peripheral states who participate in these institutions are dealt with by allowing some room for manoeuvre, as long as this is in the interest of the dominant social forces and their counterparts in developing states. Ideas, which challenge the ideology behind the hegemonic order, are absorbed to ensure that they do not threaten it. For instance, the notion of self-reliance or autonomous development (advocated by dependency theory), once it had passed through the policy analysis of the World Bank, emerged as 'do-it-yourself welfare programs'. The administration of such projects in rural areas was aimed at stemming the urbanisation process, thereby preventing those who cannot be integrated into the world economy from causing political and social instability. Cox (1983: 139) concludes pessimistically, that counter-hegemonic challenges via international organisations 'can be ruled out as a total illusion'.[4]

Historical structures (consisting of material capabilities, ideas and institutions) represent only part of the picture and need to be contextualised and linked to the 'historical situation.' Secondly, the analyst must also focus on the possibility of the emergence of structures that challenge the prevailing order and offer alternatives. Therefore, although the three aspects describe 'a complex reality' and may point to patterns, they are 'limited in their applicability in time and space.' In turn, the 'method of historical structures' can be applied to three points of entry; the relations between social forces centred on modes of production, forms of state (anchored in a particular state-society complex), and world orders. Again, these three may be perceived of as the three points of a triangle, which are connected by arrows indicating mutual interaction and influence. Each one of these levels (and the three taken together) reflects a specific arrangement of material capabilities, ideas and institutions (Cox, 1981: 100–1).[5]

Applying hegemony

The use of the concept hegemony in Cox's framework is not restricted to institutions. It also influences his perspective on power and change. We have already seen (Chapter 2) that Cox (1977, 1982) uses Gramsci's concept of hegemony and applies it to the international level. He is well aware of the fact that this was not Gramsci's intention: 'Not surprisingly, Gramsci did not have very much to say directly about international relations' (Cox, 1983: 124). Notwithstanding Gramsci's use of the concept at the state-society level, Cox feels that his ideas should not be frozen in time, but utilised to enhance understanding of contemporary developments. Also, Gramsci himself considered the link between state-society and international relations: 'Do international relations precede or follow (logically) fundamental social relations? There can be no doubt that they follow' (quoted by Cox, 1983: 133).

With respect to the 'neo-Gramscian school in IR' and Cox's association with it, I want to return, briefly to the genealogical question. Clearly, Cox has used his reading and understanding of Gramsci to augment his own explanatory framework. Also clearly, this understanding has influenced his conceptualisation of power (together with Machiavelli) and hegemony. But Cox is not a follower of Gramsci, attempting to apply the latter's theory to contemporary events. His, therefore, is not a neo-Gramscian perspective. He has used some insights from Gramsci, where and when they contribute to his own explanation of world order. Whether those insights are sound is, of course, debatable. But, 'The concern should be with the adequacy of Cox's understanding of the world rather than with the adequacy of his understanding of Gramsci.' (Cox, 2002: 29). I agree.

According to Cox (1983: 126–7), one of Gramsci's more important contributions was to extend the notion of (potential) working class hegemony (leadership exercised in consent with allied classes) to the actual dominance of the bourgeoisie. The hegemonic status of the latter (anchored in civil society) was reflected in the ability to rule (directly or indirectly) by extending concessions to subordinate classes. This requires a broader conceptualisation, one that recognises the symbiotic relationship between the state and civil society. The hegemonic position of a dominant class is not only reflected in the apparatus of government but also in supportive civil society institutions.

A society in which hegemony prevails, reflects the Machiavellian notion of power, '...the image of power as a centaur: half man, half beast, a necessary combination of consent and coercion' (Cox, 1982: 39–40). When hegemony prevails, coercion remains in the background, ready to be used in 'marginal, deviant cases'. Power, ultimately, has to be located in society, because the latter impacts on the arena of politics. Societies, in which a dominant class ('industrial bourgeoisie') has not succeeded in establishing hegemony, are in a condition of 'stalemate'. Gramsci termed this a situation of 'passive revolution'. These societies have absorbed some components of a 'new order', which has been externally forced on them, without the old order being displaced entirely.

This situation, drawing on Gramsci, may be characterised by one of two outcomes: caesarism or *trasformismo*. Under caesarism, a 'strong man' takes charge to arbitrate between opposing forces of equal strength, as Mussolini did in Italy, after World War I. Under *trasformismo*, a leader attempts to construct as broad a coalition as possible, and to co-opt the leaders of those groups who would challenge the interests of such a coalition. Cox regards 'Passive revolution', which is the absence of hegemony, as the state of affairs in developing countries (Cox, 1983: 129–31). The 'historic bloc' (another Gramscian concept) refers to the interplay (mutual shaping) between ideas, politics, ethics and the social relations that result from the material conditions of production. The formation of a historic bloc requires a dominant class and a state that 'maintains cohesion and identity within the bloc through the propagation of a common culture'. This is essential to ensure that the interests of the subordinate classes are also accommodated, albeit without threatening the interests of the dominant class (Cox, 1983: 132–3).

Making the controversial 'jump' to the world order level in the Coxian framework, it is the specific arrangement or 'fit' between material capabilities, ideas and institutions that point towards the absence or presence of hegemony. Cox (1981: 102–3, and footnote 24, pp. 119–20) criticises Keohane's (1981) and, by extension, Gilpin, Kindleberger and Krasner's use of hegemony. The reason being that the condition of hegemony (and its association with stability) is explained by them in terms of the (material) power capabilities of a single dominant state. According to Cox (1983: 135), hegemony (stability) is not the same as coercive dominance by one state. It also depends on whether there is a 'fit' between an arrangement of material power, a widespread collective image of world order, and institutions which are perceived to manage in the broader interest rather than at the behest of a dominant state (Cox, 1981: 103 and Cox, 1987: 7).

Therefore, the dominance (in terms of material power capabilities) of one state may not be enough to explain hegemonic stability. For example, during the interwar years American power was dominant, yet there was an absence of stability/hegemony. In contrast, the *pax brittanica* and the *pax americana* are illustrative of hegemony at the world order level, which is associated with stability and, a 'fit' between material capabilities, ideas, and institutions. The equivalent (in Gramscian terms) of the inter-state system at the world order level are 'transnational social forces' or a 'global civil society' (Cox, 1981: 105 and Cox, 1983: 136). The world order is, therefore, made up out of and can be described in terms of social forces, as well as in terms of the interactions between states. The latter are at the interface (in a permeable sense) between transnational and domestic compositions of social forces in a specific country.

Hegemony at the world order level, usually emanates from powerful states where a dominant class has succeeded in establishing it at the national (state-civil society) level. This can only happen after a society has passed through and consolidated significant socio-economic changes. Hegemony is not only state-based, but involves transnational social forces (transnational managerial class, see below) that are linked via their relationship to the dominant mode of global production (Cox, 1983: 136–7).

In the peripheral states, however, hegemony wears thin and is more 'laden with contradictions'. This is because developing states are inclined to reflect the dynamics associated with passive revolution, although they do attempt to follow the hegemonic 'model' exported by dominant states. This involves attempts (with varying degrees of success) to incorporate the technological, economic and cultural components of the core, as well as the associated political form (liberal democracy) (Cox, 1983: 136–7).

The enduring concept of world order

In the *Millennium* article, Cox (1981: 107) focuses on the *pax americana* and evaluates it as an example of a world order. He asks how hegemony has been perpetuated in this order, and considers the forms of state and social forces within it, which could bring about its transformation. In the process he identifies two contemporary trends, the 'internationalisation of the state' and the 'internationalisation of production.' He then argues that the structural characteristics and requirements of the *pax americana* world order are linked to the internationalisation of the state. The ideological/normative aspect (ideas) of this order puts forward the need for an open international trade system, but with states retaining the right and ability to protect their populations from the negative effects of international trade.

In order to facilitate trade, the system was supported by an international monetary order in which exchange rates were fully convertible. Stability was ensured through the fixed exchange rate system based on the linkage of the dollar to gold ($35 = 1 ounce of gold). These norms were applied and monitored by international institutions such as the General Agreement on Tariffs and Trade (GATT) and the International Monetary Fund (IMF) (Cox, 1981: 108, Cox, 1987: 255, see also Eichengreen, 1996).

This world order is also characterised by the essential coordination of policies between the major (supportive) industrialised states. Policy coordination as a characteristic of the system became entrenched through the G-7 (Canada, France, Germany, Great Britain, Italy, Japan and the United States) and, the Organisation for Economic Co-operation and Development (OECD). The need to make national policies more sensitive to the dynamics of the international economy led to the increasing importance of state ministries that were more 'outward' orientated for instance, finance, the treasury, trade and the office of the head of state. Networks emerged between these government agencies and corporations, which were more, integrated in the world economy. In this way, the internationalisation of the state came about (Cox, 1981: 108–9).

Cox (1981: 109–10) argues that the internationalisation of production accompanied the process described above. This refers to sourcing and making the various components of a product in different geographical locations, after which they are assembled in the region from where they are marketed and sold. This is international production for international markets, or in contemporary terms, global production for global markets. International production takes place with control over the process in the hands of the corporation or its affiliates, through foreign direct investment. Technology and the ability to sustain technological innovation are of crucial importance. Although the actual 'arrangement' of production may differ (for example, joint ventures or alliances), ultimate control rests with the originator (patent holder) of the (applied) technology (Cox, 1987: 244–5).

Cox (1981: 110) acknowledges the increasing role of finance capital in the directing and planning of global production. In PPWO

(1987: 267) he observes that '...international finance is the pre-eminent agency of conformity to world hegemonic order and the principal regulator of the political and productive organization of a hegemonic world economy.' The question as to whether global finance has become more important than global production as the driving force of the current world order is, of course, also relevant to Cox's own emphasis on production. Cox addresses this issue in an article where he discusses Susan Strange's contribution to the study of IPE (Cox, 1992c).

In the article, he expands on his view of the role of finance set out in PPWO. Its influence over production lies in its ability to politically influence states to follow macroeconomic policies that have an effect on what is produced and for which market (domestic or export). Corporations are also dependent on it for the acquisition of new technology. Finance is, therefore, the economic form of power over the (political) modes of social relations of production. Cox (1992c: 180–1) then distinguishes between the 'real economy' (production) and the 'symbolical' one (finance). Commenting on the importance of finance in Susan Strange's work he suggests that it is the *relationship* between finance and production that is important, rather than debating which one of the two should be prioritised. In the end, they are interdependent. The state and the real economy depend on the well being of society. When the symbolic economy starts delinking from the real economy, productive capacity is reduced. This happens '...when credit at the top behaves in unpredictable and unstable ways, feeding on itself rather than nourishing the real economy' (Cox, 1992c: 181). The consequences of 'paper profits' uncoupled from productive capacity can be catastrophic. This was in evidence in, for instance, Mexico (1995), the Asian financial crisis (1997), the dramatic decline of 'new economy' corporate shares during 2000 and, the sub-prime mortgage crisis in the US that led to a global credit crunch (2007).

The internationalisation of production results in the emergence of a 'transnational managerial class.' The members of these social forces are a class 'both in itself and for itself.' The existence of this class can be witnessed in the actions of individuals, the ideology which is propagated, and the institutions, which represent its interests. The directors of multinational corporations (MNCs) and the staff of international organisations concerned with economic governance are one component of this transnational managerial class. They interact with state managers of government agencies and ministries with an outward orientation, as well as with national companies that are linked to the global production structure. Their interests are articulated through *inter alia* the Trilateral Commission, whereas probably the best illustration of their global network is the annual meeting of the World Economic Forum at Davos, Switzerland (Cox, 1981: 111; Gill, 1990).

The transnational managerial class represents the interest of those integrated into the world economy. Their interests and those of national companies diverge. For instance, the latter are more likely to pressure the state to enact protectionist policies. Similarly, the work force can be divided into those who are globally integrated and those who are not. Established labour works for globally orientated companies and is highly skilled or skilled. Non-established labour is low skilled and normally unorganised (Cox, 1987: 263). The proportion of those who are marginalised from the global economy is far higher than those who are integrated. In Southern Africa the figure ranges between 60 and 80% (Leysens, 2006). This segment is not formally employed and earns no regular income. According to Cox, they are a potential source of instability: 'A major problem for international capital in its aspiration for hegemony is how to neutralize the effect of this marginalization...so as to prevent its poverty from fuelling revolt' (Cox, 1981: 113).

When considering in which directions a future world order might move, Cox (1981: 113) argues for a focus on emerging 'social forces' which will result from the changes in the way we produce goods and services. Writing some twenty-five years to twenty years (PPWO) ago, his discussion of a potential new hegemony approximates in some ways the characteristics of the contemporary world order (circa, 2007). Cox's (1981, 1987) 'internationalisation of the state' and 'internationalisation of production' terminology pre-date the scholarly and popular use of 'globalisation' during the 1990s[6] and his conceptualisation of the hyper-liberal (globalised) state form in PPWO accurately reflects the dynamics of contemporary globalisation.

The origin of the hyper-liberal state lies in the economic crisis of the 1970s. The decade began with 'Nixon's surprise' (the decoupling of the dollar from gold) and moved swiftly into the 1973 oil crisis.

The ensuing inflation experienced in core states resulted in increased corporate pressure to do away with automatic wage increases, full employment policies and welfare transfers. Companies argued that to remain competitive in an inflationary environment, government expenditure (and therefore the rate of taxation) had to be brought down. The crisis brought about a revision of the idea on which the Keynesian state rested and, 'the social contract that had been the unwritten constitution of the neo-liberal state's historic bloc was broken in all the advanced capitalist countries in the year following 1974–1975' (Cox, 1987: 279–81).[7] Cox goes on to discuss the effect of this crisis on states, social forces and world order and thereby illustrates the value of his explanatory framework in contemporary terms.

The policies of the hyper-liberal form of state are restricted monetarism (to reduce inflation), cut backs on government spending, wage stabilisation, a reduction of welfare transfer payments to subordinate economic groups, technology intensive production for a global market, flexible employment, the erosion of tripartism (institutionalised cooperation between state, capital and labour), and a decline in social subsidies. This form of state confronts those with whom the welfarist state sought consensus, public service workers, welfare recipients and organised labour (Cox, 1987: 283–8).

Together with changes in the form of state, came changes in the social relations of production. The dominant class reflects the composition of the transnational managerial class (see above); global corporations, national industries who are integrated into the global production structure, global finance (investment houses, speculators, and banks), the state class in developing countries and, an established highly skilled work force. Those who are subordinated and are therefore potential challengers to the ideology of the hyper-liberal form which underpins the dynamics of globalisation; are semi-skilled or downscaled skilled workers as well as contract workers in the core states. In the peripheral states subordinate social forces are industrial workers, state employees and, peasants and urban marginals (Cox, 1987: 401).

Regarding subordinate social forces in peripheral states, Cox (1987: 387) speculates that 'Possibly the potential for revolt arising out of the social relations in the production process is greater in the Third World than in the advanced capitalist countries.' He sees the increasing gap between the integrated and the marginalised, as 'potentially destabilizing for the social and political order.' However, he also acknowledges that this potential is reduced by the fact that they are mainly concerned with 'survival and adaptation.' They are, subsequently, difficult to mobilise for collective action and are prone to succumb to clientelism. In the sense that they pose a threat to the more privileged social forces related to production, the state would act to repress or co-opt them (Cox, 1987: 388–9).

Where do we need to look to determine whether there is a potential for change or a counter-hegemonic challenge? Cox (1987: 393) concludes that we must focus on the emergence of social movements and that transformation may be possible 'because of a dissatisfaction with the prevailing order'. Furthermore, to investigate the potential of mobilisation the analyst must identify divisions in society which are the result of changes in the production process and 'their modes of perceiving the world, and of their potential directions of movement' (Cox, 1987: 403).

Additionally, because hegemony at the world order level expands from states that have managed to establish hegemony at the national level, the problem of change and counter-hegemonic challenges (from developing states) must also be addressed within the 'national context' (Cox, 1983: 140). In peripheral states this would mean the effective mobilisation of disaffected industrial labour in alliance with marginalised social forces. Bearing in mind Cox's scepticism regarding the ability of international institutions to mount a counter-hegemonic challenge, he concludes that, 'In short, the task of changing world order begins with the long, laborious effort to build new historic blocs within national boundaries.' (Cox, 1983: 141).

Accessing social forces through modes of social relations of production

The concepts of dominant and subordinated social forces (classes which emerge from forms of production relations) need to be understood within the context of Cox's (1987) typology of 'modes of social relations of production'. In PPWO, he identifies these modes from historically observed regularities of behaviour and not, as in scientific Marxism, from inevitable progressive laws (Cox, 1987: 396). Within these modes, which must be historically located, we see reflected the power relations (between dominant and subordinate classes) that emanate from production. Cox's modes present us with potential doors through which we can move (as a first step) to identify and access the understandings of contemporary marginalised groups and how they fit into and interact with states and world orders.

How do social relations of production come about and what criteria does Cox use to identify the different modes? In accordance with the notion of social power, *the power relations prevalent within society determine what is prioritised in term of production*. This also has an influence on *how* it is produced (who controls the process and who actually produces). The 'structure of authority' (division of labour) reflects the role of dominant and subordinate social forces. Lastly, social relations of production are also centred on the *distribution* of the benefits of production, who gets what, when and how? A mode of social relations of production can also be identified according to its intersubjective content. This is the shared understanding that people have of the dynamics of a particular mode. Building on research completed while he was at the IILS (with Harrod, see above), Cox bases his identification of twelve modes of social relations of production on the reciprocal relationship between three dimensions (objective, subjective and institutional) and the factors associated with each one (Cox, 1987: 11–12, 17–29).

Before outlining each mode, we need to take note of two points that Cox (1987: 32–3) emphasises about them. First, different modes can co-exist. They do not exist in isolation, nor do they follow each other successively. Modes that are dominant during a certain historical phase become subordinate and adapt themselves to changes in (social) power relations. They may keep most of their characteristics, and simultaneously reflect new ones, which have been developed to integrate the mode with new forms. Second, analogue modes may exist. They can be found in state-society complexes which differ from the ones in which the mode originally developed. The mode is, so to speak, 'out of place'. For instance, the urban poor of cities in industrialised states have much in common with the marginalised component of cities in developing states. However, the different political economic context within which the mode finds itself requires us to make a distinction.

The first four modes are related to the 'simple reproduction' characteristic of the 'pre-capitalist era.' This phase involves no significant changes in the movement from one production cycle to another. There are no changes in the social relations of the producers, nor is there any significant change in production output (except when natural phenomena intervene, such as drought). All four modes have survived (albeit in adapted form) in societies that have undergone capitalist development. The modes are: subsistence agriculture, peasant-lord agriculture, the primitive labour market and household production (Cox, 1987: 35).

The subsistence mode of production survives (in adapted form) among a substantial proportion of the population in developing states. It relates directly to contemporary rural marginals. Its distinguishing feature is that the producers, '…are substantially outside the monetized economy and the networks of commodity exchange.' Production is aimed at self-sufficiency. The term 'subsistence', Cox (1987: 37) cautions, does not refer to the level of consumption. This mode of production is rooted in social relations that are based on kinship and lineage. It is not an expansive mode, in the sense that surplus is produced for a larger market. The motivation for production and distribution is based on custom and communal solidarity. The mode has adapted itself in societies that have undergone capitalist development by supplying migrant labour to urban areas. The repatriation of wages serves as an additional source of income. In this sense, the subsistence mode is indirectly connected to the national and globally orientated sector of the economy (Cox, 1987: 36–9).

The peasant-lord mode of production survives in adapted form in some developing states. In its pre-capitalist form this mode involved the collective organisation of people by a political authority. The dominant class appropriates surplus agricultural production. Historically, this class has based its right to appropriate on military capacity, religious justification, or by ensuring that peasants remained in monetary debt to them. The peasants are bound to land that they do not own and have no direct access to markets to sell their produce. The institutional form is one of direct domination. In its modern form, the dominant class has maintained its hold by keeping peasants indebted. The political power of large landowners (for example in Latin America) is derived from a state which supports their dominant status and which has declined to intervene on behalf of the peasants. However, the need for efficient commercial agricultural production for world markets has put this mode of production under increasing pressure (Cox, 1987: 39–44).

In the primitive labour market mode of production, people become detached from the social relations that bind them to production (e.g. the subsistence mode). This mode developed during the pre-capitalist phase but survives today as 'predominantly a phenomenon of poor and newly industrializing countries of the Third World' (Cox, 1987: 45–7). Again, a major proportion of marginalised social forces in developing states fall within this mode of production. As the number of people in the subsistence mode decline, the number of people in the primitive labour market increases. They are a constant indicator of the gap between the rich and poor and consist of landless labour, casual wage earners, and hawkers. They engage infrequently with the dominant mode of production. Although they are prone to sporadic outbursts of violence, the contemporary state can control them because they lack cohesion. Usually there is no class-consciousness, no institutionalisation, and no organisation among them, or between them and the state.

Because they do not have any social cohesion or the security associated with the subsistence mode, people in this mode are highly insecure. They may attempt to remedy this insecurity by looking for protection in tribal links, ethnicity, gangs or criminal networks. The intersubjective consciousness of this group is characterised by a fluctuation between instrumentalism (aimed at survival) coupled to passive acceptance. Outsiders can potentially use their underlying dissatisfaction to ferment revolt. In return for votes and to maintain political stability, governments will tolerate their informal settlements and, '...keep the bulldozers away from their lean-to's or run a source of electric power into a squatter's settlement' (Cox, 1987: 48).

The last mode of production in the 'simple reproduction' era, which also remains in contemporary capitalist development, is the household mode. This mode has no class structure, but depends for its division of labour and its authority relations on (religious) myth. It is a mode, which is supportive of all the other modes in the sense, that it reproduces and sustains the work force. In some rural areas of developing states this mode of production combines with the subsistence mode. In contemporary capitalist societies, the household mode of production is under pressure because of developments in the other modes. Women, who, due to myth and convention, are the primary producer/manager of the household, often hold part-time jobs in other modes of production. The productive function of the household has been greatly reduced, but during times of unemployment it remains 'the producer of last resort' (Cox, 1987: 48–50).

The next eight modes of production are all associated with modern capitalist development. Whereas Wallerstein (1974) starts his analysis of the development of capitalism in the sixteenth century (based on the expansion of trade and the accompanying accumulation of capital), Cox (1987: 51–2) focuses on the development of a particular form of capitalism from the beginning of the nineteenth century. This form is characterised by '…an organization of production designed to generate the expansion of capital'. The early phase, 'competitive capitalism' reflects two modes of production, the self-employment mode and the enterprise labour market.

The self-employment mode of production consists of the independent, small-scale, owner who, with the use of his own and his family's labour, produces goods and markets them. In the past this was the artisan who resided in the city, and the independent tenant and freeholder farmers who had managed to extract themselves (through the peasant revolts) from feudal obligations. The contemporary version of this mode includes independent farmers, artisans, writers, shopkeepers, professionals, writers, consultants, and craft market peddlers. They work within a market, which is dominated by other modes of production, and produce goods or provide services which large companies find too expensive to enter into. The contemporary globalisation friendly state holds out self-employment as the entrepreneurial solution for the unemployed. Only some succeed, however, as '…most forms of self-employment are precarious in the long term' (Cox, 1987: 52–5).

The formation of the enterprise labour market mode of production is associated with the migration, in Europe, of landless labourers to the cities where they worked for wages. Wage labour is, however, not only a defining feature of modern capitalist development. Before the development of industrial wage labour, artisans or merchants would hire or 'put out' the production of goods and services to 'cottagers' who eventually ended up as wage earners. Importantly, and accompanying the development of this mode, was a change in production which was characterised by capital accumulation and re-investment for market production, production of tradeable basic goods (food and clothing), the commercialisation of land, and the creation of a 'pure' (unregulated) labour market where wages follow supply and demand and workers are separated from production means (Cox, 1987: 55–7).

This state of affairs (cf. Polanyi, 1957) resulted in a vast unskilled supply of labour for the early phase of industrialisation in England and, later, attempts by philantropical industrialists and the unions to 're-humanise' the unregulated labour market through state imposed regulations which were aimed at re-embedding the market into society. Initially, the state sided with employers and punished attempts by labour to react through organised resistance. From 1850 onwards in England, two streams (based on the levels of skills) of workers could be discerned, '…a more established category of industrial workers and another category less established or more precariously connected to permanent industrial employment' (Cox, 1987: 59–60).

In contemporary terms, union and state regulations do not cover many workers. They form a version of the enterprise labour market today, more accurately described as 'non-established enterprise labour'. These workers are low or semi-skilled, they do not belong to unions, and their employment is insecure. They can be found in small to medium private enterprises that are associated with the 'sweatshops' in the clothing, footwear and electronics trade in developing states (the majority are often women). When they are employed by larger industries, their situation is more precarious than that of established labour. Their employment is often of a temporary nature (for example, standing in for permanent staff), or otherwise they work for companies to which larger industries 'outsource' work such as cleaning, maintenance and security. When they do belong to unions, or are covered by some state regulations related to their work status, they are usually less protected than established workers.

The last four modes describe types of institutionalised arrangements between social forces and the state. The last mode within the phase of competitive capitalism is Bipartism. This mode emerged in England from 1867 onwards and is associated with the need to stabilise modern capitalist development. It involved the institutionalisation of the relationship between established trade unions and management, supported by a state that felt that its political base was secure enough to grant concessions to labour without endangering the established political economic order. This was a sign that hegemony had been attained at the national level. In return, established industrial labour, through its industry-based trade unions, agreed to accord legitimacy to the capitalist order. In the bipartist mode, the state does not intervene to influence the outcome of employer-labour disputes, and the latter are not interested in influencing government policy (Cox, 1987: 63–9).

The next three modes of production developed after the advent of monopoly capitalism (initiated by the depression of 1873–1896). The post-depression rise of large corporations was essential for the development of enterprise corporatism as a mode of production. In this mode, management enters into a 'symbiotic' relationship with labour. The idea of an essentially conflictual relationship is passed off as being a 'misperception' on the part of labour. Instead the enterprise corporatist mode of production emphasises harmony and the company becomes an extension of the community.

The welfare and security of the established labour component and their families is the primary concern and focus, while company loyalty and worker participation are encouraged. Where trade unions exist, they are enterprise unions, and they do not concern themselves with unemployment and working conditions outside of the company, and certainly not with the problems of non-established workers. The important issues for enterprise unions are career advancement, health and welfare issues, and pension payouts. The companies are usually aligned with state economic policy, and there is, therefore, no significant intervention by the state. Contemporary examples are the Japanese *zeibatsu* and South Korean *chaebol*, as well as large public companies (Cox, 1987: 70–4).

In tripartism, the state is more concerned to influence the outcome of settlements reached between managers and trade unions. The increasing complexity of macroeconomic policy and management at the state level, brings about a change in outlook, 'Governments were no longer prepared to leave wages and employment questions entirely to the interaction of employers and unions' (Cox, 1987: 74). This mode became prevalent after WWI. The sacrifices and contributions made by labour and capital during the war, led to demands for mutual consultation and compromise on matters related to macroeconomic policy. The keyword is 'persuasion' rather than 'domination'. This form of (elitist) economic interest group interaction dilutes democracy, but in the final resort governments can always appeal to the people to pressure the other 'partners' into making concessions. The tripartist mode requires an organised labour movement and an acceptance by labour of capitalist hegemony (Cox, 1987: 74–8).

The last mode of production that Cox (1987: 79) associates with late industrialisation (in developing states) is state corporatism. This mode is found in societies were there is an absence of hegemony ('passive revolution'). The state uses coercion to force industrial development in the absence of hegemonic consensus. No cooperation between management and labour has evolved and the institutionalisation of relations between economic interest groups is 'imposed from above'. State power is used in the national interest, to prevent instability and to promote industrialisation. There is no effective democratic counterweight, in the form of parliament or civil society, and trade unions and employer organisations operate under state supervision. In their dealings with the state, they work through bureaucrats and the 'party elite'. This mode usually includes large corporations and a national trade union (controlled by the state) and excludes the enterprise labour market, primitive labour, peasants and self-employment. Its aim is social control by the state (Cox, 1987: 80–1).

After PPWO: Globalisation, civilisations and multilateralism

Two years after the publication of PPWO, Cox (1989a: 250–1) introduces the idea of the possible emergence of a 'post-Westphalian' order, which he compares to the medieval phase under the pope and emperor. In this order the state is impacted on, and co-exists with non-state forces that '...assert their own identities and claim recognition and tolerance within the world system'. The (counter-hegemonic) future world order that Cox now foresees is a multilevel one where the state co-exists with other authority centres (at the sub-national and transnational levels. A single 'dominant hegemonic universalism' does not support this order. Instead power will be diffused and the order will be based on the acceptance of civilisational diversity. Globalisation, although dependent on the principle of territoriality to enforce market rules, also results in an increase of centres of authority at the micro- (regions within states, such as Flanders in Belgium) and the macro-levels (inter-state regionalism, for example the European Union). States, micro-regions, macro-regions and 'global cities', therefore reflect a world order that is similar to the multilevel order of medieval Europe (Cox, 1992a: 306–9 and Cox, 1993c: 278).

The notion of a post-Westphalian world order and the long-term viability of the state as an autonomous actor in the global political economy is continuously emphasised by Cox during the early 1990s (see Cox, 1992b, 1993b, 1995a). He qualifies this, however, by noting that 'There is, of course, no question of the state disappearing.' (Cox, 1993d: 35).

Cox's interest in 'civilisations' dates back to his time at McGill University as a History student. He explains that, 'The attempt to recover the sense of the spirit behind the historical is what motivates me to explore the idea of civilisations.' (Cox, 1999b: 392). His deliberations on the possibility of a post-hegemonic order lead him to conclude that it is unlikely that a new hegemony will replace the contemporary declining hegemonic order. The reason for this lies in the difficulty of finding '...an archimedian point around which the new order could be constructed' (Cox, 1992b: 140–1). One can no longer assume that a future world order should or can only be based on the universalist tenets of Western civilisation, he argues. Instead, 'mutual recognition' will involve moving '...towards a kind of supra-intersubjectivity that would provide a bridge...' between civilisations. This post-hegemonic order would be one in which (culturally) different intersubjectivities would co-exist (with their own values and development strategies), while 'supra-intersubjectivity' would be the base which connects and reconciles them (Cox, 1993b: 265). These points are reiterated when Cox (1995b: 9) argues for a return to the study of civilisations, not in the manner of Huntington's 'clash of civilisations' premise, nor by accepting Fukuyama's 'end of history' thesis, but in order to find common ground.

One issue, for instance, which has been subject to 'inter-civilisational' debate, is the notion of human rights. Can Western, Asian, African and Islamic conceptualisations of human rights be reconciled with each other? Or, more generally, can we move from different local/national intersubjectivities related to different 'traditions' of civilisation, to a supra-intersubjectivity which represents the coming together of norms which the various traditions share? (Cox, 1996a: 147). Cox (1995b: 26) suggests that the elements of a 'supra-intersubjectivity' might be found in the fact that everyone shares the same eco-system and that we are all affected by environmental decline, that it is in everyone's interest to reduce global inequality, that we all recognise that violence is a sign of the breaking down of communication, and that we realise the importance of consensus on the issue of human rights. The emergence of a possible supra-intersubjective civilisational tradition would, however, be rooted in the plurality (diversity) of co-existing traditions (see Cox, 2002).

On globalisation, Cox (1993a: 204) observes that the market is dislocated from national societies, and that it depends on an extremely small base for its legitimacy. The mobilisation of the marginalised would result in a confrontation between democracy and market efficiency, but notwithstanding their size, the 'fragmentation and powerlessness of these groups would make the task formidable'. Cox, therefore, reiterates his caveat on the potential of transformation from below made elsewhere (1981, 1987). Nevertheless, he stresses that a successful counter-hegemonic challenge will have to be anchored and arise from within 'popular strata'. Such a challenge will emanate from local reactions to the problems of globalisation (provision of welfare and (re)organising production). He predicts that these reactions will be aimed at local authorities and to 'collective self-help', rather than at the state. This is due to the alienation and de-politicisation that the marginalised experience. Arising from within national societies, new forms of state will result from pressure by non-state social forces. To bring about change at the world order level, this process would have to progress within a number of societies at the same time, and it would have to draw support from transnational social forces. The result would be a 'globalization embedded in society' or a 'globalisation from below' (Cox, 1993a: 207 and Cox, 2002: 40).

The 'bottom-up' emphasis is also reflected in Cox's later publications on international organisations (the return to multilateralism). This is an area of study about which he had expressed reservations and pessimism and which he maintains (Cox, 1999b and Cox, 2002: 37). The pessimism is related to the possibility of a multilateral order rooted in a 'social basis' emerging soon. It does not mean that he does not regard it as important for a more representative form of global governance. In an earlier article on the topic, Cox (1992d: 161–6) is at pains to stress that the study of multilateralism should be about more than just the institutionalised interaction between states around specific issue areas such as trade or monetary policy. A contemporary conceptualisation must interrogate the question of a multilateralism which incorporates the local and the global. Additionally, it must also include a focus on the potential for change, and not just on how the existing order is regulated. The question is whether multilateralism can include the 'level of popular forces as well as the level of governments?' (Cox, 1992d: 166 and Cox, 1996a: 153).

Cox's return to the issue of multilateralism resulted in an edited volume (Cox, 1997a). This publication emanated from his participation in the United Nations University MUNS (Multilateralism in the UN system) project. Stephen Gill (1997) edited the other volume. Cox's book re-introduces the concept 'new realism' (see also Cox, 1996a). This concept again affirms Cox's intellectual debt to the classical realism of E.H. Carr and his rejection of the ahistorical approach inherent in neo-Realism. New realism expands on classical realism's historical focus by 'broadening the range of determining forces beyond state power' and goes beyond neo-Realism's *status quo* orientation, in that it focuses on structural change and transformation (Cox, 1997a: xv–xvi).

New Realism's approach to multilateralism does not take current institutions as a given, nor does it analyse them with a view to make them function more efficiently. The approach followed is a 'structural-critical' one. It focuses on the 'normative basis for an alternative world order' by standing back from the underlying structures of the contemporary order, asking how they came about and what the potential catalysts for change are. The change envisaged is towards a more inclusive multilateralism as outlined above. Again, Cox stresses that this perspective uses a 'bottom-up' approach, aimed at '...privileging the concerns and interests of the less powerful while not ignoring the constraints imposed by the more powerful' (Cox, 1997a: xvi–xviii).

I now return to Cox's analysis of the process of globalisation and the new hierarchy it has created. He observes that the process has resulted in a division between those who are integrated, the precarious and the excluded. The last category is a 'potentially destabilizing force' that is kept at bay by 'global poverty relief' (aid and projects aimed at ensuring self-sufficiency) and 'global riot control' (intervention to stabilise states in regions which are strategically important because of their mineral resources). Furthermore, 'whole regions of Africa belong to the bottom level', and evidence shows that the populations of the poorest (also African) states are alienated from the state and international organisations which they regard as hostile instead of supportive (Cox, 1996c: 26–7; see also Cox, 1997b: 250 and Cox, 1999a: 13, 24–5).

Cox (1999a: 9) later expands, in more detail, on how he views current divisions and the concept of class. On the latter, he restates observations made earlier (see Cox, 1995a; Cox, 1996c; Cox, 1997a and 1997b). Class can no longer be regarded as a cohesive concept, which refers to a 'universal proletariat'. Dominant and subordinate groups exist, but their position in relation to a mode of production stands in a dialectic relationship to other forms of identity such as gender, religion, ethnicity, and regional affiliation. The relationship between class and identity, therefore, needs to be ascertained. Concerning the components of the hierarchy which globalisation has reinforced and created, an important point to take note of is that he views them as social and not geographic divisions. They occur globally and are not confined to the space of the core (developed states) or the periphery (developing states).

The first tier are the 'integrated'. They consist of a global managerial class who are the 'carriers of globalisation ideology' and decide on 'what is produced, where, and by whom'. They are linked to the following (subordinate) groups: middle management, technicians, and skilled workers. At the next level, Cox (1997a: 247–8 and 1999a: 9) identifies those who are precariously integrated. They are blue-collar workers who belong to 'old economy' industries, temporary workers and contract workers, all of whom are less skilled than workers in the integrated category. They are easy to replace and are segmented further by their identity consciousness. Finally, there is the category of the 'excluded'. They are not integrated (directly) into the global economy or, for that matter, into the (formal) national economy. Unskilled and unemployed they are mainly found in developing states and form the 'marginalised' sector of the population. Of them, Cox (1997a: 248) says, that they '...are a continuing source of anomic and potentially concerted violence'. Importantly, 'The marginalized and excluded remain a world of mystery because they do not seem to participate in the "rationality" of the centre' (Cox, 1997b: 247).

The elites of developing states (the state class) have generally followed strategies of incorporation into the globalised world economy and in the process national development strategies have been abandoned. The effects of macroeconomic policies in tune with what is required of the hyper-liberal form of state have brought about increased unemployment, increased crime and a reduction of state expenditures on social services and welfare. This state of affairs, Cox (1997b: 248) argues, can result in 'open revolt' or a 'passive withdrawal of obedience.' Whether societal stability can be maintained during the process of integration into the world economy, based on the policies of the hyper-liberal form of state is, therefore, an open question.

Cox regards shared ideas and collective images as the principle components of an intersubjective understanding that people have of their material world. For Cox (1992b: 138) the principal question is how the objective world is constituted and reconstructed through changes in intersubjectivity.[8] This requires a focus on the (intersubjective) ideas people have about the world and the practical problems, which arise from material challenges to their existence. If the ideas so held are conducive to the resolution of these problems, change is unlikely. However, should a contradiction arise between the ideas and the problems, the likelihood of structural transformation increases. Cox (1987: 403), therefore, emphasises the need to access the 'mental schema' of people, to determine 'their modes of perceiving the world, and of their potential directions of movement'. This need is, in fact, stressed consistently in his work (see also, Cox, 1986: 243).[9]

But herein lies the challenge for CCT and those who are attracted by it. This also applies to the critical theory in IR school. How do we move to an understanding of the 'mental images' of the marginalised? How can we access them? Following on from the discussion of Cox's epistemology, it may be possible to adapt Cox's framework somewhat to overcome this problem. Whether he would approve of this is, of course, a moot point. Any interpretation would have to be true to the essence of the historical method. I will return to this issue in the concluding chapter. To continue the process of tracing Cox's intellectual genealogy and to provide a base for comparison and deduction the next chapter outlines the development and premises of the CT of the Frankfurt School.

4
The Critical Theory of the Frankfurt School

Introduction

The aim of this chapter is to give the reader an overview of the Frankfurt School of Critical Theory (CT). This is essential in order to determine whether the association of Coxian Critical Theory (CCT) with the work of the Frankfurt School theorists is an 'honest mistake' or entirely unwarranted. A detailed discussion of the work of four scholars who (together with Cox) are usually cited as representative of Critical Theory in International Relations (IR) follows in Chapter 5.

The CT of the Frankfurt School, the Institute of Social Research (hereafter, the 'Institute'), and Habermas has been associated with the work of a number of scholars who are regarded as having initiated the 'critical turn' in IR. They are Richard Ashley,[1] Mark Hoffman, Andrew Linklater, Mark Neufeld, and Robert Cox (examples of those who make this association are Devetak, 1996; George, 1989; Hoffman, 1987; Linklater, 1992; and Smith, 1995). We therefore need to look at the origins and history of the Frankfurt School, the epistemology of CT, as well as when and how it was introduced as the 'third debate' in IR (see Chapter 5). Moreover, we also need to evaluate whether the linking of Ashley, Hoffman, Linklater, Neufeld, and Cox to the thinking of members of the Frankfurt School (see Devetak, 1996: 151; George, 1989: 274; Smith, 1995: 24 and Hoffman, 1987: 237) is valid.

Origins and history of the Frankfurt School

This section has distilled the origin and development of CT, primarily from the excellent volumes on this topic by Held (1980) and Kellner

(1989). The 'Institut für Sozialforschung' (Institute of Social Research) was founded in 1923, with private money. This, notwithstanding its formal association with the University of Frankfurt, ensured its independence. The original members and those students who were attracted to it lived during a period of turmoil, change and uncertainty in Weimar Germany. They were deeply influenced by the carnage of the Great War, the Bolshevik revolution of 1917, and the attempts to bring about a socialist revolution in Germany during 1918–1920. Many young, middle class intellectuals embraced Marxism as a reaction to the economic decline in post-war Germany. Prominent figures associated with the Institute had opposed the war from the outset, and some were involved in the failed attempt to establish a socialist republic in Germany. By the time the Institute was established, the Social Democratic Party had purged its radical elements and embarked on a path of reformism. These radical intellectuals (notably Max Horkheimer, Friedrich Pollock and Herbert Marcuse) returned to university where they pursued studies in Marxism, and later gravitated towards the Institute (Held, 1980: 16–19, 29 and Kellner, 1989: 9–10).

Kellner (1989) depicts the history and output of CT in terms of a number of chronological phases and themes. Another way to review CT is to differentiate over a period of time between the divergent thought and output associated with the scholars who were based at the Institute and are associated with the Frankfurt School. According to Held (1980: 15) one cannot attribute a unified approach to the Institute as such. However, shared assumptions, premises and ontology can be discerned (as one would expect from a school of thought) in the work of Max Horkheimer, Theodor Adorno, Herbert Marcuse, Leo Lowenthal and Friedrich Pollock.[2] Jürgen Habermas, although also associated with the 'School', is usually discussed separately. This is because his work substantially re-interprets and expands on the premises and dynamics of CT (Held, 1980: 15). Kellner's (1989) overview and analysis of the figures associated with CT overlaps with those Held regards as important contributors, although the latter also includes Erich Fromm.[3]

The first director of the Institute was Carl Grünberg (1923–1929).[4] Under his directorship, and as the 'first avowed Marxist to hold a chair at a German University' (quoted in Held, 1980: 30), the research undertaken at the Institute was rooted in the basic Marxist assumption that society can ultimately be understood by focusing on the nature of the economy as its base. Grünberg directed the work of the Institute towards the explanation of contemporary changes in German society. During his tenure there was a distinctive focus on historical and empirical research that was published in the *Archive for the History of Socialism and the Workers' Movement*. After Grünberg's retirement in 1929, Max Horkheimer was appointed as director in 1930. Horkheimer's first address, *The Present situation of Social Philosophy and the Tasks of an Institute of Social Research*, indicated a discernible change in the epistemology of research at the Institute. Like Grünberg, he emphasised the importance of both theoretical analysis and empirical research. Horkheimer, however, introduced three points that pointed to a move away from the more orthodox Marxism of his predecessor, towards the essence of what are today understood as some of the central tenets of CT (Held, 1980: 29–31 and Kellner, 1989: 13–16).

The first, and most important point raised by Horkheimer, was the need to introduce social philosophy as a framework for the understanding of society. From this point of departure follow two other observations that are derived from the way in which Horkheimer views the task of social philosophy. He stressed the importance of viewing society in its totality and the need to explain 'the fate of human beings' as part of a community and inclusive of all the 'material and spiritual' aspects which affect them (state, economy, religion, science, art, and public opinion). This endeavour could not be undertaken in terms of the traditional philosophy approach that looks at these issues in an abstract and ahistorical manner. What was required was a synthesis between philosophy, social theory and the 'specialised sciences' (Held, 1980: 32–3 and Kellner, 1989: 16–19).

Kellner (paraphrasing and quoting from Horkheimer's address) captures the point well (I have left out the original page references), 'Horkheimer claims that the positivistic view that philosophy "is perhaps beautiful, but scientifically fruitless because it is not subject to controls", verification, experiments and the like, must be rejected, as must the philosopher's prejudice that he or she is dealing with the essential, while the scientist is dealing with bare, trivial facts.' (Kellner, 1989: 17).

Following on from this are two further observations that can be regarded as important themes in Horkheimer's address. The first concerns a move away from the more orthodox Marxism espoused by Grünberg. Economic determinism is qualified when Horkheimer emphasises that the Institute would not adhere to one dimensional explanatory frameworks; '...the attempt to derive everything from an economy which is understood merely as material being is an abstract and therefore badly understood Marx' (Kellner, 1989: 19). Instead, the interaction between society, the state, the economy and people in historical context, must be focused on with the aim of determining how society reproduced itself. This is a point with which Cox, who eschews economic determinism, progressive ahistorical Marxism and one-dimensional explanations, would have no problem.

Secondly, the research program of the Institute was to be guided by a strategy of interdisciplinary materialism. This meant that Marxist political economy would have to be supplemented by other disciplines (for example, Cultural Theory and Social Psychology) to advance a more comprehensive understanding of society. For instance, why did the working class in Weimar Germany remain divided and why there was an absence of revolutionary consciousness under conditions of advanced capitalism? It also meant a tolerance for methodological diversity, and a willingness to use qualitative and quantitative techniques.[5] The vehicle for the Institute's publications was the *Zeitschrift für Sozialforschung* (*Journal of Social Research*), first published in Germany in 1932.[6] In 1933, following Hitler's appointment as chancellor, the Institute moved to Paris and, subsequently, just before the German invasion of France, to Columbia University (City of New York) (Aronowitz, 1972: xiii, Kellner, 1989: 19, 26, Held, 1980: 34 and Morrow with Brown, 1994: 98).

It was during the period of exile (at Columbia University) that Institute members first started denoting their approach as Critical Theory (CT). This was done partly because they found themselves in a radically different intellectual climate. For one, approaches which were deemed to be too close to Marxism were frowned upon and even treated with downright hostility. Secondly, they also found the uncritical acceptance of pure empiricism by the social sciences in the US problematical. Nevertheless, the period of exile and the accompanying social and intellectual challenges also coincided with a productive period of reflection and writing by the core members of the Institute.[7] It was during this time that the 'classics' of CT saw the light. Most were translated in English and published again during the 1970s, after a revival of interest in CT in Germany during the 1960s (Held, 1980: 36; Kellner, 1989: 44).

In 1936, a major research project on the family and authority was completed and published as a two-part research report called *Studies on Family and Authority*. This was a collaborative theoretical and empirical undertaking between Fromm, Horkheimer, Marcuse and Lowenthal and focused on how the economy affected families, as well as how perceptions towards authority were formed by inner family dynamics. The interest in attitudes to authority was kindled by the rise of Fascism and Nazism and the submissive response to both by individuals. In 1937, Horkheimer published his essay on 'Traditional and Critical Theory.' The distinction is sometimes erroneously noted as having been the inspiration for Cox's differentiation between 'problem-solving' and 'critical theory'. In this seminal article, Horkheimer encapsulated his thinking on the assumptions and method of the Institute's (critical) approach to research and knowledge and showed how it was different from mainstream or 'traditional' theory. The ideas expressed in his inaugural address on the need to combine philosophy, science and praxis were also set out and elaborated on (Kellner, 1989: 36–44).

Another member of the School, Friedrich Pollock, was continuing his research on the crisis of capitalism in the aftermath of the 1929 Wall Street Crash. He argued that the market (liberal) form of capitalism had run its course and that its only means of survival lay in a centrally planned economy. This could take the form of capitalist state planning or the version followed in the Soviet Union. He predicted that a free market economy would eventually require state intervention to deal with recurrent economic crises. This intervention would take the form of 'state capitalism' (of a democratic or Fascist nature) and would involve total control by the state, leaving virtually nothing to the abstract laws of the market. State capitalism, as described by Pollock, requires more (political) planning, control and intervention than the New Deal or Keynesian models (Held, 1980: 494 and Kellner, 1989: 55–61).

In the meantime the circumstances experienced while in exile and developments in Europe and the Soviet Union had significant effects on the activities of the Institute. By 1941, the Institute was in financial trouble and some of its members started working for the

US government. Both Horkheimer and Adorno moved to California, effectively bringing to an end the Institute's ability to follow a collective multidisciplinary approach. Secondly, a significant shift in thinking (inspired by Adorno) took place, which culminated in the publication of *Dialectic of Enlightenment* by Horkheimer and Adorno in 1947, as well as *Eclipse of Reason* by Horkheimer in the same year.

Both publications reflect the 'philosophical' turn in the development of CT and signalled the abandonment of the project to attempt a synthesis of philosophy, science and social theory. The lack of working class resistance to the authoritarian project of Fascism and Nazism, the excesses of Stalinism in the Soviet Union and, the use of the modern state to commit genocide led to a profound disillusionment with the instrumental reason of the Enlightenment and the science it had produced (Kellner, 1989: 83–90).

Bourgeois science and the political economy of 'progressive' Marxism were rejected as instruments of control and domination in the quest of humanity to conquer nature. The 'totally administered' society, where humans dominate humans, was the end result of this quest. As Horkheimer (1947: 59) put it, 'Positivist philosophy, which regards the tool "science" as the automatic champion of progress, is as fallacious as other glorifications of technology.' Critical reason is offered as an alternative to the instrumental reason of positivist science, although as Kellner (1989: 86) points out, what exactly critical reason is encompassed of is not really developed in *Dialectic*. In the end, *Dialectic* and *Eclipse of Reason* can be read as a radical critique of instrumental reason and positivist science, leaving the question open as to whether the foundationalist roots of the Enlightenment are rejected *in toto*, or whether its benefits need to be retained. Habermas and his followers would later confront this critique, accepting the notion of control and domination inherent in positivism, but arguing that a reconstruction of foundationalist notions of knowledge is possible (Kellner, 1989: 89).

During this time, other members of the Institute who remained in New York (among others, Lowenthal and Neumann) had embarked on a major empirical project to determine how authoritarian character traits in individuals were linked to prejudice and anti-Semitism. This study (named *Studies in Prejudice*) resulted in several publications one of which was *The Authoritarian Personality* published in 1950, by Adorno and a number of collaborators. In conjunction with a number of psychologists at Berkeley, a detailed questionnaire was sent to 2,099 respondents. The subsequent analysis identified a set of character traits or trends, which the authors associated with prejudice and conservatism (Kellner, 1989: 114–16).

Soon after the completion of *Studies in Prejudice*, an offer was received to take the Institute back to Frankfurt. As a result, Adorno, Horkheimer and Pollock returned to Germany and, by 1953, had re-established the Institute. Marcuse, Lowenthal, Kirchheimer and others remained in the US. Although the Journal was not revived, a series of publications called *Frankfurt Contributions to Sociology*, was initiated. Horkheimer did not publish anything of note in the post-war years, and Adorno (although productive) did not revisit the multidisciplinary project of the 1930s (and to an extent 1940s). Adorno died in 1969, Pollock in 1970, and Horkheimer in 1973. Although Adorno and Horkheimer's work served as an inspiration for the radical student politics of the 1960s, they were not actively involved.

It was Marcuse and Habermas (particularly Marcuse)[8] who were more directly involved in the praxis of protest at this time and who are the names most commonly associated with the Frankfurt School (Marcuse) and CT (Habermas) in the aftermath of the deaths of Adorno and Horkheimer. Marcuse, in fact, is often viewed as the intellectual father of the New Left during the 1960s. He was a committed advocate of the need for critical theorists to also become involved (based on CT's premise that the division between object and subject is untenable) in the politics of transformation and emancipation (Kellner, 1989: 119–20 and Held, 1980: 38–9).

Marcuse's work (for instance, in *Eros and Civilization*, 1955 and *One-Dimensional Man*, 1964) carried forward earlier critiques of the 'totally administered society', mass culture, art, and communications (the mass media) by Adorno, Horkheimer and Lowenthal. Essentially, these were viewed as the products of instrumental reason, producing conformity to the consumerist society that is linked to the capitalist mode of production. Marcuse (in *One-Dimensional Man*, 1964) stresses the difference between 'false needs' and 'true needs'. The former are items that people think they need because of the socialisation dynamics prevalent in a consumerist society. The latter are 'vital needs', such as food, clothes, and shelter 'at the attainable level of satisfaction' (quoted in Kellner, 1989: 160).

Although Kellner (1989: 197) refers to Habermas (and Claus Offe) as 'two of the most influential members of the second generation of the Frankfurt School', this may lead one (according to Held, 1980: 249) to view CT as an approach which cohesively developed from Adorno to Habermas. But, although there are intellectual linkages (even similarities) between Habermas and the 'inner circle' of the Frankfurt School, there are also substantial differences. These lead Held (1980) to differentiate between Habermas and the 'School', an important point to note, particularly when we go on to consider CT in IR, as well as the supposed 'linkages' between Cox and CT.

Habermas' debt to the Frankfurt School is most apparent in his early work *(Structural Transformation in the Public Sphere,* 1962 and *Towards a Rational Society,* English translation 1970). In these volumes he analysed the growth of the state and its political role (referring to its increasing autonomy) in technically administering and neutralising the problems that arise in the crises which 'late capitalist' societies typically experience. His conceptualisation of knowledge and how it relates to human activities (needs) in *Knowledge and Human Interests* (1971), however, differs from Adorno's more pessimistic conclusion on the possibility to establish foundationalist truth claims. Secondly, both Adorno and Horkheimer developed a deepseated skepticism regarding the possibility that capitalist society could be transformed. Habermas, particularly in his identification of the crises which contemporary capitalism has to deal with, seems to be more optimistic (Held, 1980: 251–3, Kellner, 1989: 196).

Notably, in *Legitimation Crisis* (contrary to Adorno, Horkheimer, Pollock and Marcuse who concluded that capitalism had managed to devise the means to ensure its own survival), Habermas (1976: 61–8, 75–92) argues that the capitalist state faces rationality and motivational crises in addition to economic crises. Essentially, economic crises (arising from class conflict) are replaced by rationality crises that relate to the inability of the state to deliver the goods and manage the economy – both of which are essential to ensure legitimacy. The motivational crisis arises when individuals are no longer inspired to act in accordance with the values that underpin the system and start to question its structures.

Furthermore, according to Habermas the system (at the time of his writing) was no longer able, through religion, ideologies of individualism, consumerism, and art and culture to provide the motivational legitimation required for its continued existence. He concluded that the possibility of a crisis that could affect the perpetuation of the capitalist system was likely. Habermas' attempts to develop a normative base for his version of CT began to take a linguistic turn from the early 1970s and reached their apogee with the publication of the two-volume *The Theory of Communicative Action* (1984, 1987) (Held, 1980: 284–95; Kellner, 1989: 196–200 and Morrow with Brown, 1994: 334).

Epistemology

This section provides a broad overview of some of the core values and premises underlying the epistemology of CT. The epistemology and method of CT are difficult to encapsulate as a single coherent structure because the members of the Institute tended to adopt their own unique formulations. Nevertheless, some key elements can be noted, with an eye on the next chapter that deals with those who use CT in the analysis of IR. I will therefore concentrate on lifting out those aspects of CT that have been used in IR by Ashley, Hoffman, Linklater and Neufeld.

The underlying value assumption of CT is to emancipate humans from all forms of domination.[9] The reference here is to emancipation from the domination that is encapsulated within the capitalist system of production and exchange. It also means emancipation from a form of science (specifically positivist science) that has been instrumental in perpetuating *status quo* power relations. These themes can be said to run as a connecting thread in CT, from Horkheimer to Habermas. Consequently, CT also attempts (not always successfully) to connect theory with practice, and envisages social-political transformation. Referring to Habermas' critical-emancipatory interest, as one of the three interests on which the generation of knowledge is based, Morrow with Brown (1994: 147) make the point as follows, 'In short, a fundamental assumption of critical theory is that every form of social order entails some forms of domination and that the critical-emancipatory interest underlies the struggles to change those relations of dominant-subordination.' The view that positivist science is *status quo* oriented, that dominant-subordinate relations emanate from the capitalist system and, the concern with transformation, resonates with CCT.

Horkheimer and Adorno (in *Dialectic of Enlightenment*) view domination as something, which emerged from the post-Enlightenment ascendancy of instrumental reason. Domination is in evidence when 'the thoughts, wants and purposes of those affected by it would have been radically different, if it had not been for the effects created by domination.' (Held, 1980: 140). In this summation of Horkheimer and Adorno's conceptualisation (and later Marcuse) of the concept, it becomes evident that domination is not only viewed as being the result of the inequalities generated by capitalism (which is regarded as one historical incidence of domination). It also arises from the need of humans to control nature, and following on from there, the need to control other humans, 'The human being, in the process of his emancipation, shares the fate of the rest of the world. Domination of nature involves domination of man' (Horkheimer, 1947: 93–4). This takes place in the form of internal domination (self-discipline), control over labour, and through science and technology.[10] Domination, therefore, does not depend solely on coercion. It is based on legitimacy and also on a process of alienation that restricts the options of humans involved in social struggles (Morrow with Brown, 1994: 10, 149).

Although CT accepts the complexity associated with various forms of domination, it does posit, in accordance with its (historical) Marxist roots, that the analysis of contemporary society cannot proceed without taking into account the dynamics and contradictions which arise from the dominant mode of production and exchange (capitalism). Nevertheless, this does not translate into economic reductionism, nor does it mean that CT is blind to the shortcomings of progressive Marxism, 'Both bourgeois science and scientistic Marxism utilized excessively objectivistic methods, and thus were not able to conceptualize current problems' (Kellner, 1989: 23). The objectivism of scientific Marxism leads to an inability to understand the subject and the absence of 'revolutionary consciousness' or to think about ways in which it could be created.

To overcome the restrictions (and associated stasis) imposed by positivist objectivism, the project that early CT embarked upon was to work toward a 'materialist social theory' (Kellner, 1989: 46–7). The components of this theory are reflected (mainly) in Horkheimer's early work. The CT project in the 1930s involved an attempt to move towards unification between science and philosophy, while at the same time recognising the differences in method between the two.

The traditional division between the disciplines and between the 'positivistic' and 'humanistic' approaches to knowledge generation in the social sciences was accordingly questioned and CT attempted to act as a bridge between both. This approach is described by Kellner (1989) as 'supradisciplinary'. Materialism, according to Horkheimer (1972: 226), stems from the material conditions within which humans have to satisfy their needs and the conflict which follows, 'Thus the critical theory of society begins with the idea of the simple exchange of commodities...' which must '...lead to a heightening of those social tensions which in the present historical era lead in turn to wars and revolutions'. It is not a metaphysical materialism that aspires to a universalist account of being, because concepts and theories are located in and are a part of historical events. As the one changes so does the other (Kellner, 1989: 28 and Morrow with Brown, 1994: 4–6).

Horkheimer also criticised approaches to knowledge that maintain a rigid distinction between subject and object. The two cannot be viewed separately from one another, because the one is influenced, in a dialectical manner, by the other. The subject (the human agent) is affected by material conditions (for instance, economic conditions), while in turn material conditions can be influenced (made or unmade) by the subject. Thought (our accounts of reality) and the objects that are our focus are contextually dependent of who we are and where we are located in history. A materialist social theory also emphasises the need to understand the structure of society in terms of its material (economic) constraints on the attainment of human 'happiness', as well as the need to change 'concrete conditions' (Kellner, 1989: 30–2).

Horkheimer is skeptical about the use of pure transcendental metaphysics because it attempts to explain human existence through intuition and offers unmediated and unattainable idealist palliatives to the condition of human suffering. At the same time the 'unconnected' facts and the supposed value free approach of positivism is also criticised. CT, while rejecting the values espoused by idealist philosophy, derives its underlying values (alleviation of suffering) from contemporary and concrete material circumstances. Its ontology is 'the reality of human needs, class interests, and the constitutive role of the system of production in shaping social reality and experience' (Kellner, 1989: 31, 35). Horkheimer's essay (1937) on the distinction between 'traditional' and 'critical theory' further concretises the main aspects of CT in opposition (but not in an exclusionary manner) to positivist science, 'Even the critical theory, which stands in opposition to other theories, derives its statements about real relationships from basic universal concepts, as we have indicated, and therefore presents the relationships as necessary. Thus both kinds of theoretical structure are alike when it comes to logical necessity' (Horkheimer, 1972: 228).

Critique of positivism[11]

Horkheimer's major concern with traditional theory is that it does not reflect in upon itself. Traditional theory (the nomological deductive model from the natural sciences applied to the social sciences or positivism[12]) does not locate ideas in society; it views itself as autonomous from the society in which it functions. Thus, 'The scholar and his science are incorporated into the apparatus of society; his achievements are a factor in the conservation and continuous renewal of the existing state of affairs, no matter what fine names he gives to what he does' (Horkheimer quoted in Kellner, 1989: 45). Traditional theory, therefore, views the anomalies of society as a part of its dynamics and not necessarily as something, which requires transformation.

CT, on the other hand, is not concerned with perpetuating the *status quo*, but to strive for a unity between theory and practice, to bring about transformation. It '…has for its object men as producers of their own historical way of life in its totality. The real situations that are the starting-point of science are not regarded simply as data to be verified and to be predicted according to the laws of probability. Every datum depends not on nature alone but also on the power man has over it' (Horkheimer, 1972: 244). Habermas would also later address the problem with 'reflectivity' extensively. In the preface of *Knowledge and Human Interests* he states: 'That we disavow reflection is positivism' (Habermas, 1972: vii).

Held (1980: 166–7) discussing the similarities between the Frankfurt School's critique of positivism and Husserl's *The Crisis of European Sciences and Transcendental Phenomenology*, summarises their position on the reflectivity problem in positivism as follows, 'It is intrinsically impossible for this science to assess its own objectives, or the purposes for which it is employed. Since it regards the world as a domain of neutral objects, as one such object itself it cannot even comprehend or assess itself; for it cannot reflect upon itself.' Moreover, the essence and purpose of positivist science cannot be explained or subjugated from within because they are linked to the 'social project' of attaining instrumentalist control over nature.

Marcuse (1941) also makes this point when he discusses the positivism of Comte. To Comte, social institutions were a given and could not be changed. He was in favour of order and stability and suspicious of revolutionary forces. Events, which were indicative of societal instability, should be isolated and subjected to scientific scrutiny, so as to resolve them. The premise that there is nothing but observable facts in which all science must be grounded, and the fact/value distinction which follows from this, means that there can be no other basis from which to critique society. Consequently, we should (generally) accept that which we can observe as given and that not much can be done to change it. Human activities become objectified under the operation of natural laws.

Marcuses' point is that this position is in itself a value judgement, and one that, in terms of its own premises, positivism cannot base on observation.[13] The result is a legitimisation and maintenance of the *status quo*. CT does not view facts 'in isolation' of the society in which they are embedded, nor in isolation of the individual who perceives them. It assumes that the facts 'out there' are 'our' facts; we cannot interact with them, without *interpreting* them (Held, 1980: 162–4). Or, in E.H. Carr's (1961: 11) words; 'It was, I think, one of Pirandello's characters who said that a fact is like a sack – it won't stand up till you've put something in it.'

Notably, the Frankfurt School and later Habermas (see below) did not propose that the results of positivist research should be ignored, or that empiricism as such needed to be rejected. The early project of the Institute was to bridge the gap between philosophy and science, and between materialism and idealism. As we have seen, some of the initial projects of the Institute used the method of survey research. The problem that CT correctly identifies is how one particular form of knowledge generation became dominant and, how it is used to perpetuate the *status quo* through its goals of prediction and, ultimately, control.

Held (1980: 187–8), summarising Horkheimer's view of the 'individual empirical sciences' and their relationship with CT, stresses that the latter must be prepared to engage with and subject its claims to the findings of 'traditional theory' (while remaining aware of the limitations thereof), 'The limitations and one-sidedness of the individual, empirical sciences are to be superseded not by rejecting out of hand experiences won through methodological research, but by reconstructing and reinterpreting their works in the total context to which their concepts and judgments refer'. (Held, 1980: 188).

Adorno, Horkheimer and Marcuse, recognised and acknowledged the emancipatory effect of positivist science in the nineteenth century. It delivered people from dogma and superstition and held the promise of also delivering them 'from natural necessity, domination by the forces of nature and drudgery in work.' (Held, 1980: 163). However, the carnage of the Great War at the beginning of the twentieth century and the subsequent economic decline (accompanied by the rise of Nazism and the ensuing Second World War) cast a shadow over progress, science and technology. Notwithstanding this skepticism (which later became more pronounced) toward 'traditional theory', Horkheimer (quoted in Morrow with Brown, 1994: 97), reflected the pragmatic approach of the Institute on this issue: 'If such a method is applied to society, the result is statistics and descriptive sociology, and these can be important for many purposes, even for critical theory.'

This point is also made by Habermas (1972: 308–11) when he discussed the three bases on which the generation of knowledge depends and how they relate to human interests. He referred to these as 'knowledge-constitutive interests' and identified three: empirical-analytic, historical-hermeneutic, and critical. The empirical-analytic form is associated with the deductive-nomological model of positivism. The cognitive interest of this form is technical control. The historical-hermeneutic form is not related to observation, but to 'the understanding of meaning'. This understanding is derived from textual interpretation and acknowledges the role of the 'interpreter' in arriving at conclusions about historical meaning and the connection with his/her own world. The cognitive interest related to this base of knowledge generation is practical (Habermas, 1972: 310).

The last knowledge base is related to 'critical social science'. Critical social science goes beyond the goal of producing 'nomological knowledge', by focusing and aiming to discover when proposed 'law-like regularities' hide ideologically determined relations of 'dependence' (domination) that can possibly be changed. Through self-reflection, the subject to which the laws are supposed to apply can be emancipated: 'The latter (self-reflection) releases the subject from dependence on hypostatized powers' (Habermas, 1972: 310). The cognitive interest here is, emancipatory.

Again, this does not entail a rejection by Habermas of one form of knowledge-constitutive interests for another (superior) one. Related to this issue, it is worth quoting in full, Bernstein's (1976: 194) interpretation of Habermas' view of the empirical-analytic sciences: 'It is essential to realize that Habermas is not criticizing or denigrating this type of knowledge. On the contrary, insofar as he claims that it is grounded in the dimension of human life that involves human survival, he is stressing its importance and its basic quality for any social life. Habermas' primary object of attack is the ideological claim that this is the only type of legitimate knowledge, or the standard by which all knowledge is to be measured.'

A critical theory of society

What, essentially, does a CT of society encompass? In accordance with the notion of self-reflection, CT aims to locate ideas in historical context. It must point out the gap between ideas and reality. This, Horkheimer proposes, can be done through the method of *immanent critique*. In practise, this requires pointing out the contradictions between the ideas/values that are propagated for a society and reality (practice). For example, the idea of market efficiency and equilibrium achieved through the pursuit of individual self-interest and the promise that this form of economic activity is fair, just, and will ultimately enhance equality and freedom. The market efficiency idea is contradicted by the reality of the continuing occurrence and perpetuation of poverty, inequality and economic crises. Ideology, so perceived, is something which needs to be historically determined by focusing on whether the universalist message contained therein conceals disharmony, is in the interests of a dominant group, and whether these contradictions are portrayed as the natural state of society.

Historical laws are different from natural laws. They are made and can be unmade by people. However, the more behaviour conforms with the idea of the reality proposed (via mass communications and culture) by the ideology, the more (in order to survive) will indi-viduals '...become agents and bearers of commodity exchange'. It will seem, accordingly, as if society functions according to universal 'natural' laws. The task of CT is to show that society can only be understood by acknowledging that 'laws' are linked to 'specific modes of human organization'. Abstracting them (as positivism does) leads to the perpetuation of the *status quo*. CT makes '...the individual and the conditions under which he or she lives the object of critical reflection...' (Held, 1980: 168–9, 183–6).

A CT of society reveals that concepts do not reflect reality. Thought and being are not identical, as Hegel believed; instead the critical theorist discovers that concepts are part and parcel of a constantly changing reality and that they therefore have a justificatory pur-pose. Concepts are therefore intersubjective; they are formed, main-tained and changed by structures and agency. Explanation, for CT, revolves around showing how theories and concepts mask relation-ships of domination (the purpose of ideology) and how they cannot encapsulate absolute truths, but are always historically contingent: 'Materialism, unlike idealism, always understands thinking to be the thinking of particular men within a particular period of time. It challenges every claim to the autonomy of thought' (Horkheimer, quoted in Kellner, 1989: 29).

In order to construct an accurate picture of society, CT (as pro-posed by Horkheimer) introduces the notion of 'mediated totality', and the need to reflect the 'synchronic' and 'diachronic' dimensions in the process of explanation and analysis. The term 'mediated totality' refers to the importance of focusing on the interaction between the different spheres of society, and to avoid the economic reductionism of 'vulgar' Marxism, while at the same time recognis-ing the crucial role that the economic sphere plays in society at large. Any aspect of society; political, social, cultural and psycholo-gical cannot be viewed in isolation but must be explained in terms of its relationship to the others, and in particular the economic. As such, the 'superstructure' (the state) is viewed as having much more autonomy, relative to the rest of society, than classical Marxism is prepared to concede (Held, 1980: 164–5).

In order to analyse capitalist society, it is important to focus on it as a system in order to recognise how and why this system has developed and changed historically both at the state and global levels. It requires a focus on the dialectics (contradictions) within and between the various spheres of society, leading to proposals for alternatives that may not necessarily be realised. Horkheimer was careful to stress that contradictions will not necessarily lead to change for the better. 'Progression' is not an inevitable historical force; it depends on the capacity of human agency to bring about change. The synchronic aspect of analysis is related to the 'research' component of enquiry. This may involve utilising the methodology of 'traditional' theory to create an accurate 'snapshot' of the structure of society in its 'mediated totality'. This must be followed by a diachronic or historical 'placing' of the findings, also referred to as the process of 'presentation'. In the process of presentation and 'immanent critique' concepts and findings are de-objectified – they are placed and re-interpreted or historically contextualised (Held, 1980: 178, 188 and Kellner, 1989: 48–9).

Some initial observations on echoes and similarities with Coxian Critical Theory

It is interesting to note that Cox spent some five years at the same institution (University of Columbia, New York) to which the Institute of Social Research relocated during its years of exile from Hitler's Germany. But apart from this coincidence, what are the similarities between CCT and the CT of the Frankfurt School?

The assumption of CT, that domination not only depends on coercion but that it is also based on legitimacy resonates with CCT's conceptualisation of power as a centaur (see Chapter 3). Cox, however, also stresses cooptation through the maintenance of a universalist ideology together with the provision of material benefits for those who are drawn in. The critique of the subject/object division in positivism by CT is similar to CCT. The subject (human agent) is impacted on by material conditions, but material conditions can be made or unmade by the subject. Ontologically, the fundamental importance of the production system in the shaping of everyday experience is also similar to CCT.

According to CT and particularly Habermas, positivism does not reflect in upon itself and regards the problems of society as anomalies that do not require systemic transformation. The quest to reveal 'law-like regularities' ignores relations of domination. The result is that the *status quo* is perpetuated. This relates to Comte's perspective that events that are indicative of societal instability should be isolated and subjected to scientific scrutiny, so as to resolve them. Thus positivism regards itself as autonomous from society. Cox would not disagree with this premise. His often quoted 'theory is always *for* someone and *for* some purpose' (Cox, 1981: 87) points to the need to reflect on the contextual origin of all theories, not just positivism. Habermas would not disagree either.

On the issue of data and facts, CT affirms that humans create facts and interact with them through their attempts at interpretation and understanding. This reminds one of Cox's inside/outside distinction that he sources from Collingwood. Positivism's claim to value freedom is in itself a value judgement, because of its inability to self-reflect on its purpose through its association with the social project of instrumentalist control over nature. Humans are thereby subjected to the laws of nature. This observation by, for instance Marcuse (1941), is also made by Cox (1981). Finally, Horkheimer's method of immanent critique, the notion of a 'mediated totality', and the essential 'placing' of synchronic profiles of contemporary society in diachronic context share much with CCT's emphasis on the necessity of locating ideas in historical context, the pointing out of contradictions between ideology and material deprivation and, the intersubjective nature of concepts which are shaped and changed by structures and agents. The critical theory of society, as espoused by Horkheimer is non-utopian and non-progressive. Change depends on the capacity of human agency. Here one is reminded of CCT's assumption that change is not inevitable and that it is constrained by the limits of the possible.

Finally, there is Horkheimer's observation that 'Materialism, unlike idealism, always understands thinking to be the thinking of particular men within a particular period of time' which reminds one of Cox's (1981: 87) 'Theory is always for someone and for some purpose' and 'There is...no such thing as theory in itself, divorced from a standpoint in time and space.'

5
The 'Critical Turn' in International Relations

This chapter focuses on how the 'critical turn' in IR[1] developed through an analysis of the earlier work of some of the scholars who have been associated with it. Primarily, the CT in IR originated as a reaction to Waltzian neo-Realism (see Chapter 3). I deal with a sample of the work of four authors who are often linked to the work of the Frankfurt School and to Habermas. They are Andrew Linklater, Richard Ashley, Mark Hoffman and Mark Neufeld. As we have seen, Cox's work is usually also linked to the Frankfurt School of CT. Consequently, Cox is often mentioned together with Linklater, Ashley, Hoffman and Neufeld, as belonging to a CT in IR school. In fact, Murphy (2007: 2) speculates that the majority of students have probably been taught that Cox's 1981/1983 *Millennium* articles signalled the start of the critical turn in IR.

The questions, to restate, are whether there are indeed any theoretical commonalities between these authors and the Frankfurt School. Secondly, whether these authors share any theoretical premises in their respective approaches that warrants grouping them together and, finally, whether there are any commonalties between their work and Coxian Critical Theory. The following sections address, in turn, the substance of the contributions by Linklater, Ashley, Hoffman and Neufeld to a CT of IR.

Andrew Linklater

Linklater's approach emphasises the need for a CT of IR to incorporate aspects of various perspectives, so as to provide an all encompassing framework which is able to give an empirical account of how to move toward the goal of human emancipation. According to Linklater (1990: 4) the main approaches in IR, 'have overlooked the possibility of a critical theory of international relations which analyses the prospects for universal emancipation'. His earlier work explicitly aims to connect a CT of IR to the Frankfurt School and more specifically to Habermas. He regards Cox as an example of someone who not only points out the shortcomings of mainstream approaches in IR, but who actually uses a CT framework to analyse historical 'paths of development' and to assess the possibility for emancipation (Linklater, 1990: 27).

In a review article published in 1986, Linklater sets the scene for his 1990 volume, *Beyond Realism and Marxism: Critical Theory and International Relations*. He argues that neither Marxism nor Realism can, in isolation, provide an adequate account of IR. Marxism is criticised for not considering the effect of inter-state relations ('diplomatic and strategic interaction') on state-building, and on the development of capitalism and the process of industrialisation. Realism is taken to task because it abstracts the inter-state system and its operation from other spheres (society and economy) and concludes that its characteristics have endured historically. Its prescriptions are therefore aimed at ensuring systemic maintenance. He then introduces the notion of a critical theory of IR that has to be distinguished from the 'dominant perspectives',[2] and identifies three things it should do. First, it must envisage an 'alternative world order' based on the concepts of 'freedom' and 'universality'. Second, it must identify and explain the constraints that impede the attainment of such an order in practice. Last, it must strive to conceptualise an 'emancipatory practice' so as to move forward towards this new order (Linklater, 1986: 310).

In *Beyond Realism and Marxism*, Linklater (1990) goes on to develop a more comprehensive critique of Realism and Marxism, elaborating on what he perceives as the purpose of a CT of IR. He starts out by explicitly linking his view of the difference between 'traditional' and 'critical' theory to Max Horkheimer's distinction as set out in his 1937 essay. The critical turn in IR is, according to him, represented by his own work (1986) and, by Ashley (1981), Cox (1981), and Hoffman (1987). The historical development of theory in IR is then divided (following Martin Wight) into Realist, Rationalist and Revolutionist. Linked to these perspectives are three core issues with which each one is concerned, as well as three modes of enquiry. Realism is concerned with power, and uses the positivist method. Rationalism is concerned with order and uses the hermeneutic method and, Revolutionism focuses on emancipation and uses critical social theory (Linklater, 1990: 8–10). How does Linklater deduce these linkages and, what does an encompassing CT of IR, based on an 'incorporation and supersession' of Realism and Marxism's strong points, look like?

To start with, Linklater identifies and supports his view of epistemology (positivism, hermeneutics, and critical theory) through Habermas' three knowledge-constitutive interests (see Chapter 4). Importantly, he thinks of these three modes of thought in a dialectical, progressive manner. Rationalism is an improvement on Realism, while Revolutionism (viewed by Linklater as representing CT in IR) advances our understanding of IR beyond the shortcomings of Rationalism. It is only CT that can extend 'the human capacity for self-determination' and provide the human subject with greater autonomy from societal relations characterised by domination.

The IR link is made through the work of Ashley (1981), who associated Waltzian neo-Realism with Habermas' notion of positivism and its goal of technical control. Here we find the ahistorical approach to recurrent state conflict, which is only concerned with the *problematique* of state survival in an anarchic world. Practical Realism (similar to Linklater's rationalist approach), on the other hand, is more concerned with the meaning of 'diplomatic practice' and how states adhere to certain norms and principles in international society. This focus on meaning can be associated with the hermeneutic method. Lastly, according to Ashley, there is the approach that focuses on the possibility of a transformation of the contemporary state system. This approach is linked to critical social theory (Linklater, 1990: 9–10). Linklater goes on to consider the three perspectives and their associated core issues, and method of enquiry in turn.

Linklater regards Waltz's (1979) *Theory of International Politics*, as an example of the positivist, 'technical' method associated with Realism. It is linked to positivist science and its associated emphasis on control. Waltz's framework (see Chapter 3) rejects 'reductionist' explanations of international politics. Namely, those approaches which focus on, for instance, the impact of domestic dynamics on foreign policy. Waltz, regards the foreign policies of states as being alike because they are similar 'units' that operate in an anarchic system. Differences in state action can only be attributed to differences in power capacities. The state system should therefore be 'abstracted' from domestic politics, as well as from international economics and society.

Linklater (1990: 14–15) accepts that a focus on the 'strategic interaction' between states is essential, but argues that to abstract it from other spheres '...ignores the existence of actual or potential logics of systems-modification which may strengthen the bonds of international community'. He then emphasises that neo-Realism fails to account for its own part in 'reproducing the power relations which it regards as the objective foundation' and the fact that no universal consensus is possible in a system consisting of different states with no central authority. Following Cox (1981), he points out the need for theoretical self-reflection, which is absent from neo-Realism (Linklater, 1990: 13, 15).

Rationalism, according to Linklater, combines neo-Realism's focus on power and anarchy with a concern for the normative underpinnings that lead states to cooperate around shared principles and values. This is an outcome of its practical interest with order, consensus and legitimacy. There are, in other words, moral considerations which must also be taken into account and which act as a constraint on the actions of sovereign states. This concern with order, argues Linklater, is reflected in the work of Hedley Bull. The latter's work focuses on how international order is linked to the existence of a set of principles ('international political culture') which characterise and are essential for the existence of international society. The international system must, therefore, be explained not only in terms of power relations, but also in terms of its underlying principles. In this sense, Bull stresses the fact that perspectives on the international state system are anchored in the societies that are a part of it. This approach allows for a more historical analysis of different state systems, based on the founding principles and the consensus formed around them. Consensus on values (for instance, international economic justice) enhances order and stability, and provides legitimacy (Linklater, 1990: 15–19).

For Linklater, Rationalism (as exemplified in the work of Bull) is more concerned with the question of how an international community can be expanded from a set of principles that are 'universally binding'. For this reason it is closer to the revolutionist project which is concerned with change, and also to Linklater's own understanding of a CT of IR. International order must, ultimately, depend on norms which are universally acceptable and which facilitate the creation of a 'community of states' (Linklater, 1990: 21).

Linklater (1990: 21–5) goes on to describe what for him is a CT of IR, Revolutionism. He begins by distinguishing between the ethical criticism of Kant, the revolutionism of Marx and, the 'immanent critique' of the Frankfurt School (see Chapter 4). Linklater views Revolutionism as a perspective that is 'best explained by considering the political theory of the Frankfurt School'. He accepts the School's critique of positivism and Marxism, namely that a belief in technological progress towards eventual emancipation, carries within it the seeds of a new form of domination. He concludes, however, that its pessimism with regard to the potential of the proletariat or other social movements to achieve emancipation, led it to abandon the emancipatory project.

Habermas, who 'sought not only to recover critical theory but to do so within the Marxist tradition', Linklater argues, would later continue this project. He goes on to highlight Habermas' distinction between 'labour' and 'interaction' and, how the focus on language and culture within interaction brings in an interest in the moral development of humanity, in addition to Marx's concern with control over nature. Linklater, then emphasises Habermas' point that in an interconnected world, individuals have a dual moral identity. They are citizens of states with the associated obligations, but they also have a morality that fits the potential role of world citizen rather than 'the citizens of a state that has to maintain itself against other states' (Linklater, 1990: 26).

By focusing on the possibility of attaining universal moral principles, Habermas, according to Linklater (1990: 27), succeeds in 'recovering critical theory' and the emancipatory project, which is aimed at trying to expand the area of 'social interaction' that is subject to universal moral principles. Moreover, this resonates with the (hermeneutic) method of Bull, who also identifies the need to go 'beyond the principle of state sovereignty'. Bull, says Linklater, focuses on similar problems and issues, and this points towards a need to consider how the different perspectives must be evaluated in terms of the contribution they can make 'to one another's development.' What then, does Linklater's CT of IR envisage?

As one can see from the discussion above, Linklater anchors a CT of IR in the Frankfurt School and, more specifically, in Habermas. In fact, he regards CT in IR as significantly impacted on by the Frankfurt School's theory of society. He specifically refers to Cox's (1981) differentiation between 'problem-solving' and 'critical' theory as an example of this (no doubt thinking of Horkheimer's 'traditional' and 'critical' theory distinction). Cox's view on the need for theory to be self-reflective is viewed as resembling the Frankfurt's School's criticism of positivism. After sympathetically reviewing Cox's seminal article (1981), he then introduces Giddens to support his own contention that a CT of IR should be 'post-Marxist.' Linklater agrees with Giddens' point, that Marxism failed to account for the persistence of the state and war and that the emphasis on the proletariat in effecting emancipation towards socialism 'is incompatible with the notion that the modern world is governed by multiple logics'. Linklater concludes that Cox does not adequately address the Realist critique of an approach based on historical materialism and a focus on production (Linklater, 1990: 27–31). So, on the one hand Cox is held up as an example of how the Frankfurt School of CT has influenced CT in IR. But, on the other hand, Cox is not considered to be 'post-Marxist.'

A CT of IR must (in terms of the dialectical development of perspectives) take on board the 'achievements' of the positivist and hermeneutic methods, as well as the strengths of Realism and Rationalism. This requires a focus on power and security to assess how state interaction impedes the movement towards international community. It also requires a focus in order to show how the commitment of states to principles acts as a constraint on unilateral action. Finally, it necessitates a focus on potential and real 'developments that may strengthen the bonds of international community' (Linklater, 1990: 32). Neither an exclusive focus on 'war' or on 'production' provides the whole picture. According to Linklater, a CT of IR that is biased towards indicating how we can widen political and moral community must incorporate a focus on how the rules that govern the society of states have been established and, how universal moral principles have come about historically (Linklater, 1990: 171–2).

Linklater (1992) revisits these issues in an article[3] that restates the case for a CT of IR and ties this to the notions of 'exclusion' and 'inclusion'. He argues that the state should apply its 'universalist moral discourse' to its own practices of excluding minorities (based on class, race and gender). Normatively, a CT of IR must 'facilitate the extension of moral and political community in international affairs'. This does not mean ignoring cultural differences, but it does mean moving towards a 'post-sovereign' account of IR and assessing, empirically, what the impediments are which prevent the extension of (international) political community. This requires paying more attention to 'sub-national and transnational loyalties' and envisages the continued existence of states, but with reduced sovereignty (Linklater, 1992: 93–4).

In order to tackle the project of the extension of political community beyond states, Linklater does not regard CT as 'the next stage in the development of International Relations theory' (see Hoffman, 1987: 244). In accordance with the approach set out in *Beyond Realism and Marxism* he does not think that CT is uniquely equipped to pursue this project by itself, but rather '...when articulated fully (it) can give direction to the field as a whole...it can...shed light on what the ensuing phase should be' (Linklater, 1992: 79). He is aware of the enormity of the task that the critical theory project must confront. Additionally, he attempts to address the accusations of postmodernists, that he is promoting the establishment of a universalist international political community that is based on the norms and principles of the West.[4] To this charge, Linklater (1992: 80–1) replies that both Habermas and Foucault are concerned with questions of exclusion and, that strategies to resist exclusion must of necessity privilege 'moral universals in the end'. In the end, post-modernists' refusal to put forward any concrete suggestions, except to be averse to 'closure', seems to satisfy Linklater that his attempt to construct a 'more encompassing approach' has merit (Linklater, 1990: 88–90).

In conclusion, Linklater's attempt to construct a CT of IR is wide-ranging. It cannot succeed without including a wide variety of issues, such as 'state-building', 'geopolitics', 'war', 'the effects of commerce or production' and, 'the cultural dimensions of international relations'. Bringing together various perspectives in this endeavour is, as he admits, not an easy task. It remains unclear as to how Habermas' notion of social learning (as proposed by Linklater) will be able to contribute to resolving this problem. Linklater's CT of IR, although it stresses the importance of an empirical account on how to extend international political community or to explain why it is impeded, does not manage to deliver. This leaves the whole endeavour hanging in the air as somewhat transcendental. Specifically, when we are urged to avoid choosing between perspectives and to focus on '...how states can transcend the divisive pursuit of national security by creating international order, and transform a minimal order between states into a cosmopolitan community of humankind or Kantian universal kingdom of ends' (Linklater, 1992: 96).

Related to the 'promise of critical IR' and its inability to deliver because of its research focus which has not managed to incorporate the world of the marginalised (Murphy, 2007),[5] Linklater's (1990: 172) caveat on its potential has turned out to be quite prophetic, '...the success or failure of the critical theory of international relations will be determined by the amount of light cast on present possibilities and not just by its performance in the spheres of philosophy and historical sociology alone' (Linklater, 1990: 172).

Richard Ashley

According to George (1994: 172), Richard Ashley's contributions to a CT of IR in the early 1980s (Ashley, 1981 and 1986) '...quickened the pulse of the critical challenge to the disciplinary orthodoxy perceptibly and became something of a catalyst for the extended critical agenda of the past few years'. Like Linklater (who follows in Ashley's Habermasian footsteps), he is critical of Waltzian neo-Realism ('The Poverty of Neorealism', 1986), but wants to salvage the 'practical' or 'classical' realism of Morgenthau, Niebuhr, Herz and Kissinger to develop an alternative model which he called the 'dialectical competence model' (Ashley, 1986).[6] His critique resonates with Linklater's, but is directed specifically at the 'unidimensional' structuralist positivism of neo-Realism.

Ashley's (1981) article, 'Political Realism and Human Interests', is more directly linked to Habermas' (1972) knowledge-constitutive interests (see Chapter 4). In it, he argues that Habermas' empirical-analytic base of knowledge, which is linked to the interest of control, can be discerned in 'technical' Realism. This (Waltzian) variation took shape in conjunction with the need of US policy-makers to make sense of the Cold War international system and emphasises 'scientific rationalism', 'deductive empiricism' and research which was aimed at 'problem solving' (George, 1994: 171–2). Habermas' historical-hermeneutic form of knowledge creation is associated with 'traditional' or 'practical' Realism. This variant of Realism is more concerned with meaning and an understanding of states, power, national interest, and diplomats that is historically and contextually anchored (Ashley, 1981: 227).

In 'The Poverty of Neorealism', Ashley (1986: 256) begins his argument with a reference to E.P. Thompson's critique of Althusser's Marxism. Thompson criticises Althusser for creating a positivist model of Marxism which ended up objectifying human agency, ignoring the historical Marx, watering down the dialectical component of Marx's thought and, producing a 'mechanistic theory of capitalist society.' In the spirit of Thompson's critique of Althusser, Ashley goes on to identify the 'structural turn' in North American scholarship, as represented by neo-Realism that reflects the shortcomings of Althusserian Marxism, albeit from a state-centric focus, instead of a class-based one.

Although he associates a number of names with this movement (Keohane, Krasner, Gilpin, Tucker, Modelski and Kindleberger) he emphasises that he is concerned with the underlying assumptions of neo-Realist 'lore.' Effectively, his critique is therefore mainly aimed at Waltz (1979). The 'inspiration' for his argument is found in two post-modernists, Bourdieu and Foucault, but also in Habermas, as well as '...*more distantly* [own italics], the whole tradition of the Frankfurt School.' Ashley's critique of neo-Realism then proceeds by identifying neo-Realism as the 'scientific' reaction against classical realism. He points to the similarities between structuralism and structuralist Realism (neo-Realism) and critiques various aspects thereof, statism, utilitarianism, positivism and structuralism. Reflecting sympathetically on the work of Morgenthau and Wight (as examples of classical Realism), he concludes that the 'generative potential' of classical realism can be built on by the development of a 'dialectical competence model.'

Ashley (1986: 282–4), in accordance with the critique of positivism by the Frankfurt School, contends that the positivist view of science is an ideological commitment in its own right. It requires us to view society in terms of an 'actor model'. Ultimately, the positivist approach automatically leads the analyst to look for the (individualist) actor to which all explanation must be reduced. 'Meaning' is ultimately to be found in how individual actors view society as a set of constraints. The only action worthy of consideration is 'motivated action.' Thus, explanation must focus on the interaction between actors and the instrumental reason they use. Along with the acceptance of the positivist 'actor-model', comes the refusal of science to pronounce on values and ends, but only on the means with which they might be efficiently achieved.

Neo-Realism deals with power as something that can be determined by looking at the capabilities of states, and not as a concept that ultimately is rooted in society. Ashley (1986: 291) acknowledges that this is a conceptualisation of power which is in accordance with neo-Realism's atomistic and utilitarian model of international politics, but deems it to be an inadequate one. He proposes instead a *competence* model of power, where power does not depend on the capabilities of an actor, but on the fact that the power that an actor may or may not have is dependent on the recognition accorded to it by the community. Power is 'community-reflective', and must be exercised within the 'meaning' and 'collective expectations' of the community.

Ashley's (1986: 294) 'dialectical competence model' accordingly, he argues, is better suited to the explanation of change and to penetrate below the apparently 'commonsense' structuralist approach of neo-Realism. Encapsulated within this model is his aim to offer a more self-reflective approach to knowledge generation in IR. Notably, Ashley's competence model draws on and tries to salvage the 'usable' (more interpretative) aspects of classical realism (or practical realism, Ashley, 1981). What are the assumptions of this model?

Firstly, it needs to be able to account for the origins, maintenance, and 'possible transformation' of the 'world-dominant public political apparatus'. The latter is the balance-of-power regime, which consists of states. Ashley contends that states are produced by this regime and that their actions are acts of 'self-realization' because their identities are determined and are at one with it. Secondly, global hegemony is construed as reflective of the power exercised by the dominant bloc in the regime. This is a political economic issue, one that is ignored by classical realism, according to Ashley. The functioning of the balance-of-power regime can only be fully understood by locating it within 'the social, economic, and environmental conditions…upon which it depends' (Ashley, 1986: 294). He argues that the 'silence' on economic issues is possibly the result of a consensus within the dominant bloc of the regime, to relegate the economic within the realm of 'private' actions, thereby removing it from public (political) responsibility. This feature reflects contemporary global hegemony.

Thirdly, the competence model would have to explain the political practices of the regime, centered on resource allocation and legitimation to ensure 'the possibility conditions of the regime' (Ashley, 1986: 295). Fourthly, the competence model must be able to investigate 'the learning potential of the balance-of-power regime'. How do 'competent' statesmen utilise reserves of acquired 'symbolic capital' to improvise during crises. Fifth, the model should focus on crises and particularly on how they may act as catalysts for the transformation of the circumstances upon which the functioning of the balance-of-power regime rests, '…such a crisis might be expected to be marked by the economization of politics and the resulting loss of political autonomy *vis-à-vis* economic and technological change' (Ashley, 1986: 296).

Finally, this approach would view modern global hegemony within the context of '…a multiplicity of mutually interpenetrating and opposed world orders, some of which might escape the logic of the modern global hegemony and assert alternative structuring possibilities' (Ashley, 1986: 296). This would involve focusing on challengers to the balance-of-power order and modern global hegemony, as well as their strategies to achieve transformation so as to achieve a situation where they 'secure the widening recognition of their own ordering principles as the active principles of practice' (Ashley, 1986: 297).

To conclude this section, Ashley's major contribution to CT in IR is to be found in his in-depth and wide-ranging critique of neo-Realism, using concepts and ideas drawn from Habermas (particularly, Ashley 1981), but otherwise more loosely connected with the Frankfurt School. The rudiments of his alternative model, which stresses the need to account for change, learning, and self-reflection on accepted practices within the *status quo* as proffered by neo-Realism was unfortunately not further developed or applied to practice. This is due to his shift to, and subsequent work from within the post-modernist perspective (cf. Ashley, 1987, 1988).

Mark Hoffman

Another scholar associated with the use of CT in IR, is Mark Hoffman. Hoffman's (1987: 244) article ends by boldly stating that 'Critical theory represents the next stage in the development of International Relations theory.' This, as it turned out, rather optimistic claim led to a critical response by Rengger (1988) and a short reaction by Hoffman (1988) which is worth taking note of because it points to the difference between post-modernism and CT within the genre of critical approaches in IR. Before turning to this 'mini-debate', I briefly look at Hoffman's first article.

Hoffman (1987: 231–2) begins by pointing out that IR theory can no longer be viewed or developed in isolation from social and political theory. Secondly, that the consensus surrounding the Realist paradigm has been replaced by theoretical diversity. This was signalled by Banks' (1985) identification of the 'inter-paradigm' debate in IR. More particularly, Hoffman argues that the consequence of the demise of the Realist consensus, can be seen in the movement away from the positivist method (which does not explain) to a more 'interpretive understanding' of social phenomena (which explains, but does not 'critique the boundaries of understanding'). To address the shortcomings in both, Hoffman stresses the need for a CT that can transcend them by virtue of being 'self-reflective'. Furthermore, CT opens up the possibility for 'the realisation of human potential' through a critique of the present and the potential for its transformation.

Hoffman (1987: 232–8) goes on to set out his understanding of CT. He links CT to the Frankfurt School and particularly to Max Horkheimer's (1937) essay where he distinguishes between traditional and critical theory (see Chapter 4). The point is made that theory development is a part of social reality and shapes it. He also acknowledges CT's debt to Marxism, but points out the differences between them. Habermas is identified as the foremost contemporary intellectual associated with CT. Hoffman accepts Habermas' critique of the modern variant of reason which, in the form of scientific rationalism, has created an order in which humans are the objects of control '...and politics is about who gets what, when and how but not *why*.' (Hoffman, 1987: 234). He addresses Habermas' 'knowledge-constitutive' interests (see Chapter 4) and argues that scientific rationality (as reflected in the technical interest) should not be the only foundation of knowledge. The technical interest, together with the practical interest and the emancipatory interest, form a comprehensive CT that must lay bare the ideology that lies behind 'self-evident truths' (Hoffman, 1987: 235–6).

Hoffman (1987: 236) then identifies a number of authors who represent the critical turn in IR. Among these he cites Robert Cox, Richard Ashley and Andrew Linklater. Cox is regarded as being the closest to the Frankfurt School. Hoffman (1987: 237) qualifies this by noting that Cox '...draws *implicitly* [own italics] on the links between interests and knowledge that are central to the Frankfurt School', and that Cox's view on the nature of theory '...has important *similarities* [own italics] with the work of the Frankfurt School.' Further on in the article he admits that Cox's work 'may owe more' to Giambattista Vico and Antonio Gramsci, than to Horkheimer and Habermas. However, Hoffman (1987: 247, footnote 30) again 'pushes' the association between Cox and Habermas, when he criticises Kubalkova and Cruickshank (1986: 181) for exaggerating Cox's position on Habermas and argues that there are differences but also important similarities between Horkheimer, Habermas and Cox (see Chapter 1).

Hoffman derives 'a series of basic elements' which he regards as indicative of CCT. They are based on Cox's (1981, 1983, 1986) initial formulations of the theoretical framework he would set out in PPWO. I do not paraphrase these in full here, but will revisit them below when I discuss Rengger's (1988) response. Having conceptualised CT and CCT, as well as argued that the two are associated, Hoffman (1987: 238–44) evaluates whether the three main paradigms (Realism, Pluralism and Structuralism) measure up to the key elements of CCT. Realism is dealt with first. Both 'technical realism' as evidenced by the work of Waltz (1979), and 'practical realism' as reflected in Bull's (1977) contribution to the 'English School' are found wanting, when measured up to CCT. Similar to Linklater and Ashley, Hoffman concludes that Waltz (1979) engages in problem-solving theory and finds that state forms do not matter, but that the distribution of power in the international system does. The problem becomes one of how to survive in a system where there is no centralised authority. Whether the system is prone to change or transformation is left out of the equation.

However, practical realism fares better because it focuses on the norms and culture of the international system and investigates how states arrive at a consensus in a system without 'an overarching sovereign' (Hoffman, 1987: 239). System maintenance depends on consensus, but Bull also entertains the notion of system transformation. In the end, however, practical realism also does not 'step out of itself' to consider the ideological component hidden within the approach (how the norms, values, and rules shape the 'reality' of the system of states). By not doing so, it contributes to the maintenance of the *status quo* and ends up engaging in problem-solving. Ashley's attempt (see above) to salvage and use some of Realism's core insights cannot hope to succeed, because such an approach '...would have moved so drastically from the core assumptions of political realism that it would be a misnomer to speak of it as a critical realist theory of international relations' (Hoffman, 1987: 240).

Pluralism (as reflected in the work on international regimes, interdependence and transnationalism) is regarded by Hoffman (1987: 241) as engaging in the problem-solving approach because it focuses on system maintenance in the interests of states. He notes, however, that Pluralism was a reaction to the 'state as only actor worthy of consideration' premise of Realism and therefore finds Cox's conclusion, that they are problem-solving approaches, 'odd.' After making this observation he does not pursue the matter any further, notwithstanding the fact that Cox (1981) explains his reasons for arriving at this conclusion (see Chapter 3).

Hoffman (1987: 241–2) finds more promise in the World Order Models Project (WOMP) and in the world society approach of John Burton. WOMP considers the possibility of an alternative set of norms that could form the basis of a new intersubjective understanding of world politics. It also focuses on the development of human potential in a world where states are no longer adequately equipped to cope with contemporary issues such as fast-changing technology. Burton's approach to conflict resolution stresses the importance of self-understanding/reflection by the parties involved in a conflict. His focus on the realisation of human needs leads to the premise that states are not necessarily able to meet the identity and security needs of the individual. In both cases the focus on human potential and human needs are connected, according to Hoffman, to the emancipatory cognitive interest of CT (and by association, CCT). However, Hoffman (1987: 243) concludes that WOMP and Burton fail to address the emphasis which CCT places on historical contextualisation, '…human needs and their content cannot be ahistorically defined or determined.'

The neo-Marxist approach (Structuralism) is deemed to have the most affinity and overlaps with CCT (Hoffman, 1987: 243–4). This conclusion is based on the perceived shared intellectual roots between neo-Marxist approaches and CCT. Earlier in the article, he points out that the Frankfurt School of CT deviates from Marxism in two important respects. Firstly, it does not view the proletariat as the catalyst for transformation. Secondly, it regards technology as not having the progressive role in society which classical Marxism accords to it. Hoffman's interpretation of the 'Marxism tradition' emphasises its reaction against positivism and modernisation, but negates the fact that essentially Marxism is not anti-scientific or anti-modern. Wallerstein's world system theory is identified as an example of an approach which takes account of historical context, focuses on system transformation, overcomes the division between domestic and international politics and, identifies the structural (universal) elements of world order (a capitalist system which determines the position of any state in the world system). Hoffman's (1987: 244) only criticism of neo-Marxist approaches is that they '…lack…any substantive development of practical cognitive interests, an explicit normative element other than that which it implicitly draws from Marxism.'

I now turn, briefly, to Rengger's (1988) reaction to and critique of Hoffman's article. Rengger agrees with Hoffman that IR can no longer be regarded separately from developments in social and political theory. He then re-states and critically engages with Hoffman's 'basic elements' of CCT. These are, first, that CCT, '…questions the origins of the legitimacy of social and political institutions' and that it aims to identify the universal aspects of world order and those that are dependent on history. Secondly, that CCT envisages a normatively different order within the limits of the possible. Third, that CCT is a '…guide for strategic action, for bringing about an alternative world order' (Rengger, 1988: 81–2).

Rengger (1988: 82) singles out three aspects related to the premises listed above, 'universal to world order', 'normative utopian element' and, 'a guide for strategic action'. Contained within these, he argues, is the same form of rationalism (although weaker) that Hoffman criticises on the grounds that it is aimed at societal control and the objectification of the individual. Furthermore, thinking of 'an alternative world order' – even while taking into account the historical constraints that may impede its realisation – requires us to (rationally) consider a set of criteria that would lead to the realisation of that order. These criteria must then be used as a 'guide for strategic action'. As soon as we start doing this, Rengger argues, we move into the territory of problem-solving approaches. Moreover, the establishment and use of criteria, as well as the setting out of theoretical elements is foundationalist.[7] Citing the work of Foucault, Rorty and Williams, Rengger finds that CCT's premise that the theorist 'can stand apart from the prevailing world order' cannot be attained, because 'our perceptions of that world order are themselves in part the production of such a culturally generated grid' (Rengger, 1988: 83, 86). The work of critical (post-modernist) scholars in IR, such as James Der Derian, can therefore not be grouped together with those who accept the premises of CCT.

Hoffman's (1988) brief response (with which I sympathise) to the above critique focuses on the issues of rationality, foundationalism and universalism. He (1988: 92) acknowledges that the roots of CT's rationalism can be found in the 'Enlightenment'. It is with the one-sided use of that rationalism that Hoffman has a problem, as reflected in an exclusive focus on instrumentalism and control (thereby ignoring the other two Habermasian knowledge-constitutive interests). Rationalism must subject itself to critical self-reflection, bearing in mind that CT '...seeks to critique the development of certain forms of rationality but does not accept the radical interpretivist renunciation of reason itself'. On the charge of foundationalism, Hoffman (1988: 92) responds that CT does not need to assess itself from 'within interpretivism'. It is in pursuit of 'open-ended knowledge', which involves constant 'critical assessment' and self-reflection.

On universalism, Hoffman (1988: 93) counters that we need to 'operate at the level of universality' in order to ensure progress in social and political theory. This need not be done rigidly. CT recognises that theoretical premises are open to criticism and that reason and rationality are historically contingent. Nevertheless, the anti-universalism of the radical interpretivist position leads us to 'become dispassionate observers rather than concerned critics.' Hoffman concludes by observing that Rengger is right when he says that there is a fundamental difference between CT and the critical theory of scholars like Der Derian. However, by arguing that the latter approach offers a more comprehensive overhaul of 'intellectual and evaluative categories', Rengger also commits the error of predicting the outcome of the debate. The problem with the radical interpretivist approach's relativism is that it contains '...an element of conservatism and stops short of the aims of critical theory to change the way we talk *and act* [original italics] in the world' (Hoffman, 1988: 93–4). It is for this reason that Hoffman (1988: 92) views CT '...as the most self-reflective outpost of the radical traditions of the Enlightenment.'

It is interesting to note that Hoffman does not refer to CCT in his response to Rengger, but to CT. Perhaps is it an implicit acknowledgment on his part that the association is tenuous? Later he accepts the possibility of a 'conversation' between CT and post-modernism (see Hoffman, 1991: 184, '...we need not deny the possibility of interconnections') that led to a joint chapter with Rengger (Rengger and Hoffman, 1992). In it, they distinguish between critical interpretative theory (based on a minimum foundationalism; in other words, truth claims can be assessed) and radical interpretativism (according to which there are no independent criteria for assessing truth claims, outside of any given theory) (Smith, 1995: 28–9).

Mark Neufeld

I turn, lastly, to an overview of Neufeld's contribution to CT in IR. His argument for a restructuring of IR theory that incorporates elements of CT is probably the most accessible and well-argued example of the critical turn in IR. I will therefore focus on it in some detail, particularly because he also draws on Cox to illustrate his own notion of reflexivity that he regards as an essential element of any theory which aspires to be critical. His earlier (1992, 1993a, 1993b) work is incorporated in *The Restructuring of International Relations Theory* (1995) and it is on this volume that I will be concentrating.

Neufeld's (1995: 1–2) aim is to show why there is a lack of IR theory that is 'oriented toward human emancipation'. The answer, he argues, is to be found in the domination of the 'logic of positivism.' The solution is to overcome this domination and to restructure IR theory along critical lines by undertaking 'an exercise in international meta-theory'. In other words, by reflecting on the nature of theory itself. What encompasses a good theory? To investigate this question, Neufeld draws on social and political theory and particularly on Bernstein's (1976) work. Bernstein's approach requires moving away from positivism by focusing on an interpretative understanding of intersubjective meaning, a critique of the world constituted by intersubjective meaning and, a contemplation of change and human emancipation. Similarly (but applied to IR), Neufeld focuses on the tenets and underlying assumptions of positivism, sets out what their implications are, and why they should be transformed. To do this, he uses the method of immanent critique (see Chapter 4) and draws on 'Western Marxism (including Gramsci) and, in particular, the variant known as the "Frankfurt School"' (Neufeld, 1995: 3–7).

For Neufeld (1995: 9–12) the contemporary world faces threats to human autonomy and freedom on a global scale. International Relations theory should therefore concern itself with how minimum self-sufficient human reality can be attained in a global version of the Aristotelian polis. The latter is a 'created space' within which humans can live in equality and freedom (not their natural state). How can a world that places constraints on human autonomy be transformed? How can IR theory contribute to human emancipation? The answer lies in the promises of CT. There are three elements that are central to the 'critical tradition'. They are; 'theoretical reflexivity', the importance of agency for the process of transformation and, the use of social criticism to sustain political strategies aimed at human emancipation. The absence of these elements in contemporary IR theory can be attributed to the 'positivist logic' that is pre-dominant (Neufeld, 1995: 19–20).

What does Neufeld regard as the core elements of the positivist method? He identifies two variants of positivism, Comtean positivism and logical positivism (associated with the Vienna Circle). The Comtean variant of positivism posits that 'true' knowledge is characterised by its correspondence to observable facts. Such knowledge is objective because it has no bearing on, nor does it concern itself with, the normative questions of theology and metaphysics. Lastly, the unity of the sciences is attained by the premise that positivism can be applied equally and productively in the social sciences, as well as in the natural sciences. The positivism of Comte was modified by, among others, the contributions of the 'Vienna Circle'. Logical positivism emphasised 'symbolic logic' which contained within it three elements, the referential theory of meaning, the deductive-nomological framework of explanation and the axiomatic view of theory (Neufeld, 1995: 23–31).

Neufeld (1995: 33–7) goes on to identify three core tenets (and their underlying assumptions) that are shared by all varieties of positivism (Comtean, Vienna Circle, Popperian and Lakatosian). First, the tenet of 'truth as correspondence'. For knowledge to be reliable it must correspond to empirical reality. The assumption underlying this tenet is that it is possible to separate subject and object. The existence of a 'real' world, which lies outside the subject (researcher) can be perceived and explained by the utilisation of positivism's 'neutral observation language'. Second, the notion that the practice of science is characterised by a unified method. This is based on the assumption of naturalism. There is nothing fundamentally different between the natural world and social world; therefore the method used to study natural phenomena can be applied to social phenomena. Finally, the belief that the practice of science is value-free. This is based on the assumption that facts and values can be separated.

It is these tenets and their assumptions, argues Neufeld, which have dominated IR theory and which have therefore hindered the development of CT in IR. To demonstrate this point, he considers CT's essential element of reflexivity within the context of positivism generally and, the use of positivism in IR. For Neufeld, a fully reflexive theory must show an awareness and demonstrate a willingness to reflect on its own underlying assumptions. Secondly, it accepts that all research paradigms, in addition to assumptions and tenets, also have a 'politico-normative dimension'. Third, it allows for a reasoned evaluation of what are essentially incommensurable paradigms. In terms of the first element, positivism also emphasises the importance of underlying assumptions in theory development. It is the other two elements of reflexivity, however, which challenge positivism. Why is this so? (Neufeld, 1995: 40–1).

The acceptance that paradigms have a politico-normative dimension challenges the truth as correspondence tenet, the underlying assumption of which is that it is possible to separate subject and object. This requires an acceptance by positivists of a 'subjectless' science that is dependent on ahistorical, timeless truth criteria. A reflective approach, in contrast, stresses that the criteria which are used to determine what is to be regarded as knowledge have been developed by a research community and are therefore context bound, human standards. Moreover, these knowledge criteria are also linked to politics that determines which problems its research community should prioritise. Thus, the politico-normative content of different paradigms makes them incommensurable (their values differ and they are often developed to address different political needs and problems). There can be no neutral observation language with which paradigms with varying politico-normative dimensions can be evaluated. But this does not mean that 'reasoned assessments' about the merits of contending paradigms cannot be made. According to a reflexive CT they can be made, precisely on the grounds of their different politico-normative dimensions (Neufeld, 1995: 42–6).

Neufeld (1995: 47–57) then evaluates the 'Third Debate' in IR (the first being between idealism and realism and, the second between traditionalism and behaviouralism) that, in 1989, attempted to offer a challenge to the dominance of positivism in the discipline and (tentatively) pointed the way towards the possibility of increased reflexivity (post-positivism).[8] He identifies three possible stances in this debate and relates them to positivism and reflexivity; that paradigms are commensurable and therefore comparable, that paradigms are incommensurable and therefore incomparable and, that paradigms are incommensurable yet can be compared.

Neufeld (1995: 57–68) concludes that it is only the third position, that paradigms are incommensurable but comparable, which is truly representative of the reflexive approach required by a CT of IR. He discusses three examples that he regards as representative of the critical genre in IR, 'Gramscian-inspired neo-Marxist IR theory' (reflected in the work of Cox), post-modern IR theory, and feminist theory in IR. Although the commonality between all of these is that they are reflexive, Neufeld has a clear preference for Cox's work, although he cautions that 'it must be conceded that his intervention remains preliminary and in need of further development' (Neufeld, 1995: 60). Cox's approach is viewed as reflexive because of the distinction he makes between problem-solving and critical theory (see Chapters 2 and 3). Neufeld points to Cox's statement that 'theory is always for someone and for some purpose', which illustrates that he believes knowledge and interests to be linked. He deduces correctly that CCT views problem-solving theory as *status quo* orientated and that it serves the interests of those groups who stand to gain from system maintenance. Coxian Critical Theory is superior because, although it can contain problem-solving approaches, it also considers how a particular order came about, looks at the contradictions therein, and reflects on what the possibilities for transformation to an alternative order are (Neufeld, 1995: 58–60).

Neufeld's (1995: 60–4) review of post-modern contributions to IR[9] finds them to be highly reflective, but he expresses the same reservations as Hoffman (see above) regarding post-modernism's view of rationalism. The outcome of this view is that post-modernism rejects rationality aimed at control and '... reasoned criticism itself.' It regards the use of any criteria for evaluation (whether, for instance, the politico-normative content is emancipatory) as foundationalist and universalist. In the words of Ashley (quoted by Neufeld, 1995: 63): 'Poststructuralism [postmodernism] cannot claim to offer an alternative position or perspective, *because there is no alternative ground upon which it might be established* [original italics].' Neufeld (1995: 68–9) regards this as leading to apathy. Rival theories can be compared in terms of the political project they serve, and whether that project enhances human potential and promotes the attainment of the global polis.

Neufeld, next, turns to the role of human consciousness and positivism's interpretation of it. His major point is that it cannot be viewed outside of time and context. Human consciousness is constitutive of and constitutes social reality through intersubjective meaning. Therefore, it can transform that reality. To illustrate this, Neufeld distinguishes between the way in which positivism views human consciousness and how an interpretative approach views it. Underlying positivism's view of human consciousness is the assumption of naturalism (see above). According to 'strict behaviouralism' only observable behaviour matters. An understanding of human consciousness is only useful in the context of discovery and not justification. But, 'meaning-oriented behaviouralism' does allow for the consideration of subjective meaning in explanation. This is done through the determination of the subject's attitude by using questionnaires, surveys and interviews. In this manner, it is believed, regularities can be found by linking the attitude (as an intervening variable) to the social context and the ensuing behavioural response (Neufeld, 1995: 70–82).

The interpretive approach does not deny that behavioural regularities can be observed, or that attitudes can be linked to behaviour. But regularities so observed cannot exist outside of historical context and are, therefore, insufficient to fully explain human consciousness. To illustrate, Neufeld (drawing on Taylor) offers the example of the social phenomenon of negotiation. While there may be observable regularities in the process of negotiation in the form of the different attitudes of the participants that can be linked to their behaviour, these regularities are reliant on the very existence of negotiation as a social practice. The social practice of negotiation is reliant for its existence on the shared intersubjective meanings with which a society views it. Some societies, (for instance, Japan), place more emphasis on the attainment of consensus without confrontation than others. The practice of negotiation is therefore time and context bound, and is constituted by a 'web of meaning' (inter-subjective understanding). If we accept this, it means that the assumption of naturalism, on which positivism's 'the unity of science' premise rests, cannot be maintained (Neufeld, 1995: 75–9).

Reflecting upon the role of the interpretive approach in IR, Neufeld (1995: 91) cites Cox as one of the scholars who focuses on the question of how intersubjective meanings are constitutive of the contemporary global system and concludes that, on the whole, this approach is '...being employed to underscore the possibility of a radical, emancipatory, transformation of the global order' (Neufeld, 1995: 94).

The last element of CT which Neufeld (1995: 95) considers is the requirement that its critical analysis must contribute to 'practical political activity' aimed at bringing about emancipatory transformation. The corresponding tenet of positivism is the notion of objectivity or value-freedom, with its underlying assumption of the separation of fact and value. As an example, he evaluates the position of Michael Nicholson who offers an extensive defence of the positivist method in IR. Nicholson does not deny the existence of values, but firmly believes that they can be distinguished from scientific method. The following citation (Neufeld, 1995: 100–1) encapsulates his point of view, 'Why one wants to alter social behaviour is not a scientific question: how one alters behaviour is.'

Neufeld (1995: 101–6), however, argues that positivism has within itself a normative dimension that renders its claim to value-freedom null and void. The very fact that questions which deal with values are regarded as non-scientific and that they should be dealt with by normative theory is an affirmation of positivism's own normative content. Additionally, positivism's assumption of naturalism (the unity of the natural and social sciences) limits the possibilities for change and transformation and relegates explanation to 'problem-solving' and the perpetuation of a particular order. Therefore, whether one is *status quo* orientated or change orientated is also a normative choice.

Finally, the manner in which explanation must be arrived at (using the deductive-nomological model) is aimed at the prediction of recurrence. The goal is to account for social events through law-like generalisations, thereby enabling prediction and ultimately control.[10] But because the elements to be controlled are humans and not atoms, positivism's approach is inseparable from the social project aimed at controlling humans in the same manner that science aims to control nature (Neufeld, 1995: 103, 105). Consequently, positivism's claim to value-freedom and objectivity is questionable. Neufeld (1995: 123–5) concludes that the reaction against positivism's dominance and the restructuring of IR theory along critical lines has begun. Like Linklater, he correctly cautions that its further development will depend on whether its claims can be successfully argued within the IR scholarly community, whether it succeeds in the actual emancipation of human beings and, whether it can '...be translated into significant gains in theoretical-empirical terms.'

Some brief concluding observations on 'Roots' and commonalities

What are the common (thematic) points of departure which Linklater, Ashley, Hoffman, and Neufeld share as representatives of the critical turn in IR? The themes of transformation, emancipation, reflexivity, intersubjective interpretation, and a critique of positivism feature in the work of our quartet. All of them (Neufeld less explicitly) regard the 'Frankfurt School' of CT as a primary source for the development of a CT of IR. Both Linklater and Hoffman specifically cite Horkheimer's (1937) distinction between 'problem-solving' and 'traditional theory' in their respective arguments. Essentially, however, it is Habermas' conceptualisation of knowledge-constitutive interests that provide the theoretical departure points for Linklater, Ashley and Hoffman, while Neufeld draws substantially on Bernstein (1976).

To recap, in order to move 'beyond' Realism and Marxism (while keeping and incorporating their strong points in a new synthesised perspective), Linklater draws on the Frankfurt School and more specifically on Habermas to critique the Realist and Rationalist perspectives. This also applies to the case he makes for a revolutionist approach which is more emancipatory and which points the way towards the attainment of an international political community. Critical theory, for Linklater, is transformation orientated while other perspectives (particularly Waltz's neo-Realism) are inclined to ensure system maintenance. According to him, the critical approach in IR can also be seen in the work of Ashley, Cox, and Hoffman. His critique uses Habermas' notion of three knowledge-constitutive interests (empirical-analytic, historical hermeneutic and critical-emancipatory) to argue the merits of self-reflection and a CT of IR.

'Revolutionism' encapsulates the essence of the CT of the Frankfurt School. Linklater points to, in particular, the latter's method of immanent critique and its critique of positivism and Marxism (see Chapter 4). However, it is Habermas and his focus on dual moral identity (humans as citizens of the state and as citizens of the world) who recovers the emancipatory project for contemporary CT. In support of his argument that CT in IR 'has been profoundly influenced' by the Frankfurt School, Linklater cites the distinction that Cox (1981) makes between 'problem-solving' and 'critical' theory (thereby linking Cox and Horkheimer). Additionally, he links Cox's point that theory must be self-reflective to the Frankfurt School's critique of positivism.

Ashley uses Habermas and (more distantly) some ideas from the Frankfurt School to criticise Waltz's neo-Realism and its method of positivism. Like, Linklater, he does not want to discard the 'classical' realism of Morgenthau and others entirely. Habermas' empirical-analytical knowledge-constituting interest is linked to neo-Realism's (or 'technical' realism) interest in control and system maintenance

(Linklater, subsequently used Ashley to motivate his own use of Habermas). Traditional or 'practical' realism is associated with Habermas' historical-hermeneutic form of knowledge generation. This is preferable to neo-Realism, because it is concerned with the interpretative understanding of concepts and their historical contextualisation.

Following the Frankfurt School, Ashley argues that 'technical realism' provides us with an ahistorical view of structure in which politics becomes the technical means of control, instead of the self-reflective, critical vehicle for material and institutional change that it should be. As an alternative, Ashley proposes his 'dialectical competence model.' The dynamics of this model, he proposes, lie in its aim to offer a more self-reflective approach to knowledge creation in IR. This approach emphasises the need to investigate the possibility of transformation and to focus on crises that can lead to transformation.

The themes of transformation, emancipation, self-reflection and critique of positivism also appear in Mark Hoffman's seminal essay on the promise of CT as the 'next stage' in IR theory. Similarly to Linklater and Ashley, Hoffman links CT in IR to the Frankfurt School and explicitly to Horkheimer's distinction between traditional and critical theory. Habermas' knowledge-constitutive interests, too, are introduced and conceptualised, but Hoffman makes it clear that the technical (positivist) interest *together* with the practical and emancipatory interest should form the substance of CT. Hoffman identifies Ashley and Linklater as representative of CT in IR, while viewing the assumptions underlying Cox's work as being closest to the Frankfurt School. Although he acknowledges that the connection may be somewhat tenuous, he nevertheless insists on the link between Cox and Habermas, and subsequently lists the assumptions of CCT as 'basic elements' on the way to the development of a CT of IR.

Neufeld's aim is to encourage the development of IR theory that breaks away from the 'logic of positivism' and dedicates itself to the goal of human emancipation. His method is a meta-theoretical enquiry into the assumptions of positivism and, consequently, to point out the basic elements of a theory which is anchored in the critical approach. He notes that his intellectual roots are located in Marxism and the Frankfurt School. For a theory to be critical it must: be 'self-reflective' (focusing on the empirical but also on the process of theorising and its own assumptions); be concerned with human consciousness and intersubjective meaning and the ability of human agency to change reality; and employ social criticism in support of 'practical political activity' aimed at societal transformation. Furthermore, reflexive (critical) theory accepts that research paradigms also have political and normative aims and that they can therefore, in the final analysis, be evaluated in terms of these aims.

Neufeld regards Cox's approach as reflexive because of the distinction he makes between problem-solving and critical theory, and his observation that 'theory is always for someone and for some purpose.' He admits that problem-solving theory can be useful, but it must be subjected to the requirements of reflexive/critical theory in order to determine whether it perpetuates the *status quo* and serves the interests of those who stand to gain from system maintenance. Neufeld used the concept of intersubjective meaning to emphasise that human agency is essential for the understanding of the possibility of change/transformation. How intersubjective meanings are connected to the contemporary world order is a question, according to him, that CCT investigates in order to achieve emancipatory goals.

These concluding remarks will be taken forward to the next and final chapter that will evaluate the findings in relation to the questions that were set out in the first chapter. The final chapter also reviews some selected examples of those who have attempted to follow in the footsteps of the guru and then moves on to consider the intellectual legacy of, and way forward for CCT.

6
The Legacy of Coxian Critical Theory

This chapter returns to the questions and objectives that were set out in Chapter 1, and draws out some conclusions and implications. It will be recalled that the first problem which this book has aimed to address is the incorrect 'placing' and 'linking' of CCT. The previous two chapters focused on the history, assumptions, ontology and epistemology of the Frankfurt School of CT and also provided an in-depth review of the work of the authors in IR/IPE who are grouped together with Cox in a school of critical theory. In Chapter 2 a detailed genealogy of Cox's publications was undertaken so as to trace the influences on, and the development of his thinking. This was followed, in the next chapter, by a discussion of the assumptions, epistemology and method of his core theoretical framework. These chapters are the 'evidence' chapters and they are related to the primary goal of the book, which is to shed light on and to clarify the confusion surrounding the theoretical 'locating' of Cox's work. I turn to this problem first, in the next section.

The rest of the chapter looks at the other questions that were identified in the introductory chapter. Firstly, how well have those who have adopted the Coxian approach managed to follow in the footsteps of the guru? The answers point towards the challenges that we need to be aware of if we choose to give more than 'a nod' in Cox's direction. They also provide us with some insight into where the 'weak spot' in CCT is to be found. I proceed by briefly introducing and sketching the work of a number of authors who have engaged with and attempted to incorporate CCT. The list is by no means exhaustive or representative. The selection is subjective and based on the author's own reading(s) of, and within the field of study. The last section of this chapter considers the way forward. Can CCT act as a 'bridge' between the British and American schools of IPE? If critical empiricism were to be a potential avenue to extend the legacy of CCT even further, what research strategy would be optimal?

Coxian critical theory, the Frankfurt School and Critical Theory in International Relations

Is the association of CCT with the CT of the Frankfurt School and the categorisation of Cox's work (together with Ashley, Hoffman, Linklater and Neufeld) in a CT of IR/IPE school justifiable and correct? I argue, based on the genealogy of Cox' work which I undertook, that it is understandable but that it cannot be justified and, subsequently, is not correct. Although there are commonalties between Cox and the others who are associated with the critical approach (particularly in terms of underlying assumptions), they are not indebted to the same intellectual influences. It is, therefore, not correct to claim or argue that CCT draws on or is inspired by the Frankfurt School.

Why understandable? It is clear that there are similarities between CCT and some of the assumptions of the Frankfurt School and the work of the four scholars with whom Cox is often associated. The Frankfurt School also draws on the historical Marx and rejects economic determinism. The 'supradisciplinary' approach of the early Frankfurt School, which was later revised and left behind by Horkheimer and Adorno, emphasised the need for engagement and collaborative research between traditional (positivist) and critical theory. Later, Habermas (1972) argued for a holistic approach to the development of knowledge in which there are various knowledge constitutive bases (*inter alia* the empirical-analytic dimension) that augment one another. Horkheimer (1947) viewed subordination (and the need for emancipation) as the result of the materialist challenges which humans are confronted with. His emphasis, however, was more on the inequality arising from capitalist exchange relations than on the nature of production. Horkheimer also argues (similarly to Cox) that change arises from contradictions in society and that transformation towards an emancipated society requires feasible (non-utopian) alternatives.

The Frankfurt School points to positivism's objectification of society and its focus on problems that must be resolved within the parameters of the *status quo*. It also rejects the division between subject and object, stresses that ideas need to be historically located (they are 'the thinking of particular men within a particular period of time') and that concepts are historically contingent and therefore prone to change. The concept of intersubjectivity is used to refer to shared understandings of reality that can change. The method of immanent critique requires us to focus on contemporary prevailing (universalist) ideas and whether they reflect social realities. Finally, synchronic research must be located in the 'mediated totality' of historical context.

The above core assumptions of the Frankfurt School are quite clearly similar to some of the major underlying tenets of CCT. In fact, one could speculate that Cox probably would not disagree with any of them. Cox's distinction between critical and problem-solving theory is often linked to Horkheimer's differentiation between critical and traditional theory. This has led some to conclude that 'The debt to Horkheimer in Cox's assessment of problem-solving and critical theories is plain to see' (Devetak, 1996: 151) while others believe that CCT is 'derived from Frankfurt School sources' (George, 1989: 274). Brown (1994: 213) states that Cox 'uses Habermasian ideas in his contrast between "problem-solving" and "critical" theory.' Devetak (1996) and Hoffman (1987) acknowledge that Cox's 'inspiration' and his intellectual debt are located more in Gramsci and Vico, but continue to stress the 'links' between Cox and the Frankfurt School.

Hoffman (1987: 237) is more correct when he says that there are 'important 'similarities' between CCT and the Frankfurt School, but not when he states that Cox 'draws implicitly on the links between the interests and knowledge that are central to the Frankfurt School'. Surely, if Cox had drawn (even implicitly) on the work of Frankfurt School authors, this would be revealed by a close reading of his work and the sources he cites. It would have also been revealed in the texts where Cox himself lists those who have influenced him and who have contributed to the development of his thinking (Cox, 1996b and Cox, 2002). The intellectual genealogy of Cox's work (Chapters 2 and 3) reveals only three references to authors who are associated with the Frankfurt School; a reference to Marcuse without a reference to any of his publications (Cox, 1969), a brief in text reference to Habermas (again without source citation) in the first *Millennium* article (Cox, 1981) and, the reference to Habermas' *Legitimation Crisis* (1976) in PPWO (Cox, 1987).

Marcuse is cited as someone who stresses the importance of looking at the 'real essence' behind that which is immediately apparent. Cox mentions it in connection with the need to view international organisations in this manner. The unsourced reference to Habermas is a critical one. Cox (1981: 127) notes that Habermas has '...shifted attention away from the state and class conflict'. The citation (Habermas, 1976) in PPWO supports Cox's claim that the hyperliberal state attempts to base its legitimacy on traditional, pre-capitalist values (e.g. family and patriotism). Habermas' (1972) conceptualisation of knowledge-constitutive interests could have been used by Cox to argue that the results of empiricial-analytical research should always be historically contextualised. Three of the authors associated with CT in IR (Ashley, Linklater and Hoffman) do so. Cox does not.

Cox's intellectual genealogy reveals other sources which have influenced him and on which he draws. His sensitivity for the mutual influence between industrialisation (production), forms of state and world order is indebted to the work of E.H. Carr. The notion of the link between ideas and material conditions and the sensitivity to unfettered positivism comes from Georges Sorel. The premise that ideas always evolve within a specific historical context and that material change must be understood in terms of changes in intersubjective understandings is attributable to Sorel, R.G. Collingwood and Giambattista Vico. Cox develops his view of historical materialism from the works of the Islamic historian, Ibn Khaldun and Marx. He cites Charles Taylor to support his conceptualisation of intersubjectivity. The importance of production and the social forces that are related to modes of social relations of production, as well as the importance of the dialectic approach (contradictions) are drawn form the historical Marx.

The idea of synchronic and diachronic time frames and Cox's understanding of historical structures is sourced from the work of Fernand Braudel. From Antonio Gramsci comes the idea of hegemony and counter-hegemony, a concept that Cox uses in his endeavour to understand change and transformation at the state and world order levels. Gramsci (with Carr) also influenced Cox's thought on the nature of the state. Entities such as state and civil society are not regarded as autonomous but need to interact with one another in an attempt to establish hegemony. Hegemony is maintained, not only through coercion, but also by establishing consensus. Cox's own value preference for social equity is rooted in Edmund Burke's conservatism – particularly his 'organic and solidaristic vision of society'. But he makes it clear that he distances himself from '...those who have appropriated it [Burke's conservatism] to cloak an egoistic defense of acquired privilege' (Cox, 1979: 416).

Can we associate Cox's work with Ashley, Linklater, Hoffman and Neufeld? Are there enough similarities (shared assumptions and intellectual roots) that justify grouping them together into a CT of IR school of thought? What essentially, to recap, is the purpose of these four pioneers of the critical turn in IR?

The early work of Richard Ashley is anchored in Habermas' (1972) conceptualisation of knowledge-constituting interests. Ashley used Habermas to criticise Waltz's (1979) 'structural' or neo-Realist approach and compared it to the empirical-analytical knowledge-constituting base. The 'technical' interests of neo-Realism are control and system maintenance. He rejects the 'neutralisation of human agency' (object-ification) and the resultant inability of neo-Realism to explain structural change. The positivist method advocated by Waltz and its focus on rational, objective actors is a value choice in itself, which results in an ahistorical view of international politics. States are not unitary actors. We must incorporate and account for domestic or societal power. Ashley argues for a more 'self-reflective' approach that incorporates economics and a focus on crises that can lead to transformation. Finally, classical Realism (as represented in the work of Morgenthau and Herz) and associated with the historical-hermeneutic knowledge base should be retained and incorporated in a 'dialectical competence' model.

Linklater's work (see also Linklater, 1998) is firmly rooted in Habermas and to some extent, Horkheimer. His main (normative) concern is to move from a system based on order between states to one where universal principles are established to create an inter-national (post-sovereign) political community. He views critical theory (as opposed to other perspectives) as an approach that is orientated towards transformation and suited to achieve the goal of human emancipation. Waltz's neo-Realism is singled out as inadequate because of its association with positivism, system maintenance and lack of self-reflection. While acknowledging that inter-state relations are important, Linklater argues that an exclusive focus on state power negates the norms related to the concept of international community. The difference between a CT of IR and other approaches is related to Horkheimer's traditional-critical theory distinction. Linklater cites Cox's (1981) critical/problem-solving distinction to argue that the Frankfurt School has significantly influenced CT in IR.

In a similar vein, Hoffman links CT in IR to the Frankfurt School and explicitly to the Horkheimer differentiation. Transformation, emancipation, the need for self-reflective theory and a critique of (Waltzian) positivism are themes featured in an article that regards critical theory as the 'next stage in the development of International Relations theory'. Habermas' knowledge-constitutive bases are brought in, but Hoffman emphasises that the technical interest (positivism) together with the practical and critical-emancipatory interest, must be retained in a CT of IR. This reflects Habermas' own view. As noted, Hoffman 'pushes' the link between Habermas and Cox and regards the assumptions of the latter's work as being closest to the Frankfurt School (even more so than Linklater and Ashley). Interestingly, Hoffman (1987: 240) criticises Ashley for wanting to 'salvage' classical realism because such a revision '...would have moved so drastically from the core assumptions of political realism that it would be a misnomer to speak of it as a critical realist theory of international relations.'

The central theme of Neufeld's argument is to convince us of the need to break away from the 'logic of positivism' and to move to a theory of IR that contributes to the goal of human emancipation. Critical theory must be self-reflective (looks inwards on its own assumptions; it must accept the notion of intersubjective meaning, the ability of human agency to change reality, and; it must apply its social criticism in support of political practice. Paradigms have political and normative aims and can (even if they are not commensurate) ultimately be evaluated in terms of these aims.

The bulk of Neufeld's volume is dedicated to criticising the three core assumptions of positivism, the fact/value distinction, the separation of subject and object, and the unity of science principle. Ultimately, the ahistorical criteria of the positivist method determine what problems are placed on the research agenda. These are usually related to control and system maintenance. After evaluating various approaches to the study of IR, Neufeld concludes that Cox's theory is truly reflexive because it acknowledges that 'theory is always for someone and for some purpose.' Lastly, Neufeld admits that problem-solving theory can be useful, but only if subjected to the requirements of critical theory. Change can only be understood from the vantage point of intersubjective meanings that constitute and change social practices. This, according to Neufeld, is the question which CCT focuses on.

The similarities which can be identified between Ashley's earlier work, Linklater, Hoffman and Neufeld (to a lesser extent) are centred around their explicit linking of a CT in IR approach to Habermas (1972) and the Frankfurt School (specifically Horkheimer's critical and traditional theory distinction). They also stress the need for theory to be self-reflective and criticise the positivist method that leads to system maintenance. The neo-Realism of Waltz (1979), in particular, bears the brunt of their criticism. Excluding Ashley, the other three acknowledge (in various ways) that positivism has a place in a CT of IR, but with the caveat that its results must be incorporated within the self-reflective 'spirit' of critical theory and also that they must be historically located. Linklater and Hoffman attempt to forge or stress the link between Cox and Habermas (Hoffman) and Cox and Horkheimer (Linklater).

As with the Frankfurt School, it is apparent that there are some shared assumptions between the four's understanding of what a CT of IR should be and CCT. They are: the need for theory to be self-reflective, the requirement that ideas and concepts must be historically located in order to explain change and, the critique of positivism (or problem-solving theory) which focuses on the fact/value distinction and the separation of subject and object. There is also the shared concern with human emancipation and the need for transformation towards an order that will facilitate this. It should be noted, however, that Cox does not use the term 'emancipation' (he has no objections against those who do).[1] His normative inclination is towards transformation that will bring about 'social equity.'

Based on these similarities, can we group Ashley, Linklater, Hoffman and Neufeld together with Cox in a school of critical thought? My answer to this question is no, because their intellectual debt is owed (mainly) to Habermas, while CCT rests on the eclectic incorporation of a number of diverse sources. Habermas is not one of them, nor are any of the other authors associated with the Frankfurt School (Chapter 4). In Cox's own words, 'Perhaps because the term "critical theory" came naturally to me it was assumed that I had borrowed it from them.' Regarding the tendency to compare CCT with the Franfkurt School he states, '…it would be wrong to consider the one derived from the other' (personal communication, 31 March 2007). The attempt to link Cox to Habermas and the Frankfurt School, therefore, does not rest on solid foundations but on coincidental similarities.

Hoffman's critique of Ashley's project to incorporate or 'salvage' classical Realism illustrates the problem that is encountered by those who wish to categorise Cox. In PPWO, Cox (1987: 399–400) points out that, although the departure point of his framework is production relations, '…the crucial role, it turns out, is played by the state'. The state is regarded as having had an influence on the shaping of the nature of production relations and its continued existence, though not in the same form, is not in question (Cox, 2002). In his later work on the movement towards a 'post-Westphalian' order, Cox acknowledges that the state has become one of many centres of power and that its autonomy has been much reduced. Nevertheless, he does not foresee that the state will disappear (Cox, 1993d: 35). Cox does not discard the classical realism of E.H. Carr (not Morgenthau), yet Hoffman (who had argued against Ashley that it cannot be 'salvaged') views CCT as the most representative framework of a Habermasian inspired CT of IR.

It seems that one of the crucial differences between Cox and the four CT of IR authors, is to be found in their different conceptualisations of the role of the state. Ashley, Linklater and Hoffman view Habermas as the inspiration and intellectual foundation for CT in IR. Cox (1981: 127), however, criticises Habermas because he had 'shifted attention away from the state and class conflict'. Linklater foresees a post-sovereign international system, while Hoffman is critical of Ashley's endeavour to retain some aspects of classical Realism within a more critical framework.

Richard Falk (1997) has a point when he groups together and discusses Cox, Hedley Bull and E.H. Carr under the name of 'critical realism.' All three can be regarded, in a sense, as loners. To restate

Cox's view on the attributes of the loner, 'Loners live on the margins. They may have an unconventional background...Loners tend to define their own issues and their own conceptual frameworks...One risk for a loner is inadvertently to become a guru...' (Cox, 1992c: 178–9).

Following in the footsteps of the Guru?[2]

The critical turn in IR (during the latter part of the 1980s) found its inspiration in the work of Habermas and argued for its incorporation into a CT of IR. Scholars associated with its development viewed Cox's work, mistakenly, as a commendable example of a Habermasian and Horkheimerian inspired CT of IR. An example, they argued which could (with some qualifications) act as a point of entry for those who wanted an alternative to the mainstream approaches in IR. They were, however, primarily followers of the Frankfurt School and Habermas, and not Cox. Those who have attempted to follow Cox, in contrast, are generally referred to as neo-Gramscians or (rather quaintly) the 'Italian School' (Germain and Kenny, 1998: 3). Undoubtedly, the categorisation of his followers (and his own work) as neo-Gramscian is rooted in the 1983 *Millennium* article, 'Gramsci, Hegemony and International Relations: An Essay in Method.'

Cox draws on and derives from Gramsci his understanding of how hegemony functions at the international level (Chapter 3). He came to this Gramscian-inspired approach to hegemony from a concrete situation (his subjection, at the ILO, to a US-led hegemonic idea on the nature of labour relations). This is a feature of Cox's approach: begin with 'what is known' and then move on to a theory that offers a plausible account of the event (personal communication, 23 October 2007). The 'openness' to different theories from different disciplines, so as to arrive at the optimum elucidation of complex social phenomena, is another characteristic of CCT. Herein lies its eclecticism. If this is a feature of the work of the 'neo-Gramscian' followers of Cox, as Murphy (1998: 424) points out it is, they would be exhibiting an 'attitude' (to quote Cox in a reflection on Susan Strange's death, 1999c) to his work of which, I think, he would approve. But is the 'neo-Gramscian' label useful? Given the eclectic undercurrent of CCT, it seems to confuse more than it elucidates.

This is illustrated by the friendly exchange between Germain and Kenny (1998) and Murphy (1998) on whether it is theoretically justifiable to apply Gramsci's notion of hegemony to the international level. It is interesting that Germain and Kenny (1998: 4, 16) note that Robert Cox has come to his understanding of world order via a number of sources (among others, Gramsci) and that, in a personal communication, he states that he does not regard himself as belonging to any school, 'Gramscian-inspired or otherwise.' This comment must be seen in the light of Cox's 'fugitive' theory he developed from a variety of sources. They nevertheless persist in placing him 'among new Gramscians.' Did Cox draw on Gramsci for his understanding of hegemony? The answer is, yes. Should the robustness or weakness of CCT be evaluated and measured in terms of how close a follower he is of Gramsci? The answer, I think, is a definite no.

Germain and Kenny (1998) argue that those who they identify as belonging to the neo-Gramscian school in IR are stretching Gramsci's intention with the concept of hegemony when they apply it to the international level. They also find the neo-Gramscian's interpretation of Gramsci's historicism and his take on the subject-object dichotomy to be flawed. On the 'internationalisation' of Gramsci they claim (justifiably) that his notion of hegemony focuses on the state and its adjunct, national civil society. Therefore, 'state = political society + civil society' and not, 'international state = global political society + global civil society (Germain and Kenny, 1998: 15–17). To avoid this 'stretched' reading of Gramsci they plead for a more contextual analysis of his work which takes account of meaning and interpretation. This is good advise for those neo-Gramscians who are followers of Gramsci rather than Cox (see for instance, Stephen Gill below who has engaged in a close reading of Gramsci's work). But for those who are inspired by CCT, Murphy's (1998: 417) suggestion may be more appropriate, '...we should keep our focus more on understanding *international relations* than on understanding Gramsci.'

The world has changed and transnational institutions and agents have grown exponentially since Gramsci's time. Although there may not be a global equivalent of the national state, there are transnational institutions and social movements that are engaged in the maintenance and the countering of hegemonic ideas, using the strategies of leadership, cognitive processes, coercion and consensus-building. States through multilateral institutions such as the IMF, WTO and World Bank, public and private national decision-makers and the collective groups of national and transnational civil society can choose to resist, adapt or to accept these ideas. The crucial question to consider in conjunction with explaining hyper-liberal (or any other form of) hegemony at the world order level is, of course, also whether national hegemony has been established. This will determine how any state-society complex within its own historical context will engage with a hegemonic world order. Ultimately, counter-hegemonic strategies at the national and world order level are linked.

Perhaps it is prudent to give Cox (1983: 141) the last word on his use of Gramscian-inspired hegemony, 'In short, the task of changing world order begins with the long, laborious effort to build new historic blocs within national boundaries.' This is not a negation of the state-society complex by any means. Does the 'internationalisation' of Gramscian hegemony enhance our understanding of contemporary developments at the world order level? Without neglecting the importance of the national (state) point of entry, I think Cox (1983, 1987) manages to illustrate that it does. There can be no definitive reading of Gramsci. Interpretation and meaning will depend on the context and perspective of the reader. As Cox (2002: 29) puts it, 'The pertinent question is not: Did I correctly understand Gramsci? Rather, it is: Do the inferences which I have drawn (perhaps incorrectly, but I am not ready to admit that) from Gramsci help towards understanding the historical phenomenon that is the object of my enquiry?' In other words, CCT must be evaluated in terms of how well it explains concrete situations in its own right.

For better or for worse, Cox's 'followers' are nevertheless grouped together with him in a neo-Gramscian school and one way of ascertaining who they are is to look at some of the names associated with it. Germain and Kenny (1998: 3–4) provide a useful list of authors 'broadly inspired by the Gramscian turn in IR'. Among those, the work of Gamble and Payne (1996) and Gill (1990 and 2003) will be referred to below. Space prohibited the compilation of an exhaustive and representative list. For instance, the excellent contributions of Murphy and Augelli (1988), Murphy (1994) and Mittelman (2000) are not included. The latter's work is possibly one of the better examples of the eclectic 'attitude' which underlies Cox's approach. It crosses disciplinary boundaries, offers a multi-faceted explanatory frame-work and focuses on marginalised social forces. Then there is also the risk of including authors who do not regard themselves as members of any school or followers of Cox. Moreover, the reading of their work is a subjective and context-bound exercise. In this sense, what follows below is based on our own reading and understanding of Cox. It provides a 'snapshot', nothing more.

Our reading was guided by a number of criteria. Broadly speaking, it is possible to distinguish among those who are sympathetic to the underlying assumptions and focus of CCT and give a nod in its direction; those who selectively apply aspects of CCT to augment their explanation; and those who have attempted to comprehensively apply the 'nuts and bolts' of CCT in order to shed light on a specific concrete issue. The underlying assumptions and focus of CCT can be summarised as: a focus on change/transformation; a non-deterministic approach to the interaction between agents and structures; a reflexive view of theory; an awareness of the importance of historical contextualisation; the equal importance of both ideas and material conditions in the explanation of change; the non-deterministic interaction between social forces, states and world order; and the need to access the intersubjective understanding which collectivities develop in response to their material environment (the historical method).

The 'nuts and bolts' of CCT can be encapsulated as: the acceptance of the unity between subject and object as a means of understanding change; the idea of global hegemony (based on consensus and coercion) and the possibility of counter-hegemonic challenges; a broad-based conceptualisation of production; the concept of historical structures within which social action unfolds and which consists of ideas, institutions and capabilities; and the notion of a hierarchy of modes of social relations of production (for instance, marginalised, precarious and integrated). With the assumptions and the 'nuts and bolts' as our guidelines we now turn to a discussion of some of CCT's followers. The very fact that we can do this is testimony to the fact that Cox has become an example, a teacher, and, 'inadvertently', a guru who has attracted a following. On the one hand, I think he is probably satisfied that his work has inspired others, but on the other he might be wary of the development of a Coxian 'school' or approach. With respect to this, it should be noted that we are not evaluating the contributions below in terms of who 'gets Cox right' and who does not. Apart from showing that Cox has attracted a following, this section also wants to derive some observations related to the challenges involved in the use of CCT.

Andreas Bieler has engaged with CCT both on a theoretical level (Bieler and Morton, 2001; Bieler and Morton, 2004) and practical level by applying it to a concrete situation, viz. the consideration of Swedish and Austrian social forces in European enlargement within the context of globalisation (Bieler, 1998; Bieler, 2000; Bieler, 2002). Bieler and Morton (2004: 106) correctly point out the difference between CCT and the CT of the Frankfurt School and Habermas, 'Hence, Cox may not explicitly understand himself to be working within the fold of the Frankfurt School.' But the implication of this observation seems to be that he does so, 'implicitly'. Bieler's work is aimed at providing a non-mainstream (neo-Gramscian) explanation of European Union (EU) enlargement and to use CCT as the foundation for a historical materialist analysis of European enlargement (e.g. Bieler, 2002).

The starting point for Bieler's (2000, 2002) analysis is the production structure and social forces (labour and capital) of countries in his case-study. Social forces are, however, conceptualised more along the Marxist notion of class. Class identity is a given (related to one's position in the production structure) and the trade union is the institutional expression of this collective identity. His purpose is to show the importance of a class-based analysis of EU enlargement, but not so much to identify the contradictions (the gap between ideas and material reality) in the broader European project. Gramsci's notion of hegemony is applied more to the European level than at the world order level. In this respect, ideas are regarded as important, but they do not form an essential part of the explanation. What, for instance, are the collective images and/or intersubjective understandings of Swedish and Austrian social forces (viewed as trade unions) on a market-driven approach to EU enlargement? The 'fit' between ideas, institutions and capabilities which are essential for hegemony at the world order level and how this relates to the EU 'neoliberal project' are also not considered. Ultimately, support or opposition to EU membership by organised labour and capital in Sweden and Austria is determined by material interests. These interests are determined by whether these groups are nationally (anti-membership) or transnationally orientated (pro-membership).

Andrew Gamble and Anthony Payne (1996: 1) set out (via an edited volume) to '…assess the origins, significance and likely evolution of the trend towards regionalism within the world order of the 1990s.' They focus on the link between the trend towards regionalism and world order. The latter is viewed as post-hegemonic and it is claimed that regionalism has been a response by states to the decline of US hegemony since the early years of the 1970s. The prevailing form is 'open regionalism', which is optimal for engagement with economic globalisation. To investigate this claim, CCT (viewed as 'neo-Gramscian') is chosen as an alternative and superior explanatory framework to mainstream approaches that are rejected because of their inadequate conceptualisation of power and their inability to explain change. In contrast, CCT emphasises the importance of both ideas and material interests. To this effect, the authors state that they aim to focus on the role of ideology in the shaping of a regional identity on the basis of CCT's premise that institutions are the outcome of collective human action. Other elements of CCT which are deemed to be of importance to the topic of regionalism and world order are its historicism, its reflexivity, its focus on historical structures, and the fact that it has combined the strong points of a number of other perspectives in one framework.

Interestingly, Gamble and Payne (1996) distinguish between regionalism (state driven) and regionalisation (driven by social forces within states). This, together with the stated intention to focus on ideas and their bearing on regional institutions, is an important deductive insight. This insight is, however, not followed up on in the subsequent contributions (which do provide a thorough historical contextualisation). The ensuing chapters which deal on various regionalist projects focus on states and the role of state elites, notwithstanding the fact that all of them stress the importance of ideology. Instead, the material aspect (the benefits of being open to economic globalisation) is privileged and regionalization (in which social forces are the important agents) is neglected. Nevertheless, the authors point out that regionalist state projects interact with social forces and world order. But whether and how social forces resist or support regionalism is not addressed. Relatedly, possible contradictions (the harbinger of change) between the ideology that underlies 'open regionalism' and the material benefits are not investigated either.

The Gramscian notion of hegemony is elaborated on in some detail with respect to the contemporary world order and others that have preceded it. Change in historical structures is focused on in terms of US hegemonic decline and in terms of how this is related to the increase in regionalist projects. Regionalism is a response to a non-hegemonic world order. The world order and regional (state-based) levels are therefore considered in terms of the interests of the dominant states (consensus being absent), but social forces related to production are left out.

Stephen Gill's name appears in most anthologies and citations on the Gramscian turn in IR and he has made a significant contribution to the theoretical development of the neo-Gramscian approach. In doing so, he has drawn on Cox (Gill, 1990), collaborated with him in the MUNS project (Gill, 1997), but also developed his own understanding and interpretation of Gramsci and Braudel (Gill, 1993a; 1993b and 2003). In the latter publications it is clear that he has closely read Cox and is strongly influenced by him. To this effect, some aspects of CCT remain 'points of departure' in his work. Nevertheless, through his own reading of Gramsci and Braudel he has managed to develop a distinctive approach. In a co-edited volume (with Isabella Bakker, 2003a) he has effectively argued for an expansion of Cox's focus on power and social forces related to production, to also incorporate social reproduction. This necessitates not only a focus on the state and market but also on the institution of the family (Bakker and Gill, 2003c: 25). The 'new intellectual space' that Bakker and Gill advocate is an eclectic framework that emphasises the necessity of a local focus ('fundamental social processes') (Bakker and Gill, 2003b: 3). Elements from CCT which are referred to are social forces related to production (and social reproduction), the 12 social modes of production, contradictions, historical structures, and world order.

The volume on the Trilateral Commission (Gill, 1990) uses a conceptualisation of 'transnational' historical materialism which closely follows Cox (1981, 1983, 1987). Coxian Critical Theory is thoroughly discussed, and then used to criticise mainstream approaches to IR (Liberalism and Realism). Thereafter the focus turns to the Commission as an institution that, it is argued, plays a crucial role to ensure that the hegemonic 'fit' between ideas, capabilities and institutions in a capitalist world order is maintained. The activities of the

Commission are discussed in great detail, but the analysis does not move below the world order level. The 'organic intellectuals' of the Commission (a private forum where issues which impact on the common interests of Western Europe, Japan and the US are identified and analysed) form a transnational class which represent the interests of global capital in the area of ideas. It is their task to ensure that the idea of transnational economic liberalism dominates at the world order, state and societal levels. Social forces at the state-society nexus, however, are not dealt with in much detail.

Notwithstanding the importance that is attached to the role of ideas, the explanation is inclined to favour the material side of the equation. The dominance of an idea and/or the nature of an institution are viewed in somewhat deterministic terms as the result of material power capabilities. The material (economic and military) dominance of the US confers ideological power on it. The 'consensus' or legitimacy aspect of hegemony is noted as important for the long-term survival of any hegemonic order, but is not considered in much detail in this volume. Nevertheless, a good case is made for the 'fit' between the structural power of capital, the idea of economic liberalism and the role of transnational 'organic intellectuals' at institutions such as the Trilateral Commission. How ideas, institutions and material capabilities in a world order mutually influence one another is, however, not addressed, nor is the notion of how intersubjective understandings are related to structural change.

The 1993a edited volume is a serious attempt to theoretically develop the Gramscian approach to IR (particularly, Gill's chapter on 'Epistemology, ontology, and the 'Italian School', 1993b) and to suggest a research agenda for it. Gill emphasises that Cox should be regarded as the pioneer of the approach advocated in the book (he places him on a par with Marx, Braudel, Gramsci and Polanyi). But, although the contributions that follow mostly acknowledge Cox at the start, they continue by primarily engaging with Gramsci's work. This is not surprising as, after all, the title of the book is 'Gramsci, Historical Materialism and International Relations'. The edited volume that resulted from the MUNS project includes a chapter by Cox. Gill's introductory chapter sets out the guidelines which feature in the ensuing chapters and these reflect, also, the concerns of CCT: the explanation of structural change; a concern with social equity; the importance of historical contextualisation; and the equal importance of ideas and material conditions in the explanation of change.

In *Power and Resistance in the New World Order*, Gill (2003) points to the contradictions inherent in the global expansion of neo-Liberal globalisation. The book draws heavily on the premises of CCT (the focus on contradictions, the role of historical structures, hegemony and counter-hegemony, ideas, and social forces) but engages more directly with Gramsci and Braudel. There is a multi-faceted approach that also draws on cultural power, literature and art in support of the argument. Primarily, Gill argues that the process of market-led globalisation lacks the ability to build consensus around a 'common-sense' idea that is essential to establish hegemony. Furthermore, it depletes environmental resources and the material resources that the state needs to provide public goods. Therefore, the contemporary world order is post-hegemonic and more reflective of Gramsci's 'passive revolution' (Chapter 3). The fit between ideas, institutions and 'processes in movement' (Gill, 2003: xiv) at the world order level is coming apart and this has opened up the possibility of resistance and the development of a counter-hegemonic project.

Change at the world order level is accepted as related to, and as emanating from changes at the societal (state-society complex) level. The interaction between these levels is, however, not made clear enough. This notwithstanding the stated importance that is attached to accessing the intersubjective meanings of people to understand change and social reality. Social movements (for instance, the Zapatistas) are referred to in passing and although the topic is resistance and counter-hegemony, the agents (subjects) involved in this process are not a core part of the analysis. The reason for this is that hegemony at the world order level is the main focus and not hegemony and social forces (related to production) at the state-society complex level. Production as such, is also not considered, but rather the structural power of capital.

Taylor's (2001) book on South Africa's post-Apartheid foreign relations is a comprehensive application of CCT to a concrete problem. He manages to show how hegemony at the world order, state, and social forces level are linked in his explanation of why post-Apartheid foreign policy is characterised by 'contradictions and ambiguities'. In doing so he illustrates the link between ideas, institutions and material capabilities and moves from the concrete to the conceptual. The book explains why the African National Congress (ANC), South Africa's ruling party in waiting (at the time) and leading party in the Government of National Unity, adopted a neo-Liberal orthodox macroeconomic policy in spite of its intention to follow an interventionist and redistributionist strategy. This decision accommodated the interests of national and transnational elites, but, over time estranged the party from its marginalised constituency and left-of-centre coalition partners. The impact of this decision is illustrated through an investigation of South Africa's relations with a number of multilateral organisations. Taylor draws mostly on Cox (1987, 1989a and 1999a), but also on Stephen Gill and Kees van der Pijl for his conceptualisation of hegemony.

The argument hones in directly on change and contradictions (ANC macroeconomic policy) and shows how this is linked to pressure from transnational capitalist classes at the world order (sourced from Cox), and from national political and economic elites at the societal level. Ideology and material interests are argued and shown to be connected. For instance, some South African corporations spent considerable amounts of money to bring together neo-liberal intellectuals for the purposes of drawing up 'planning scenarios'. Taylor shows the interaction between the world order and state-society complex to illustrate the pressure that was put on the ANC to follow the neo-Liberal orthodoxy. Both the IMF and World Bank provided familiarisation courses for key ANC officials and leaders.

The prevailing neo-Liberal idea at the world order level impacted on the form of state that took shape in post-Apartheid South Africa. A 'passive revolution' type evolved, where national hegemony is not attainable because of the 'contrast image' of society between the ruling outward-orientated elite and the nationally captive marginalised sector of the population. Institutions are regarded as essential to maintain the fit between ideas and material capabilities, although the analysis devotes more space to the consideration of ideas/ideology. The institutional case studies of the WTO, Cairns Group, Non-Aligned Movement and the Commonwealth are regarded as supportive of the contemporary world order. Taylor, other than noting that the marginalised are opposed to the neo-Liberal orthodoxy in South Africa's macroeconomic policy, does not consider modes of social relations related to production. The importance that is attached to the change of thinking among the ANC elite approximates CCT's notion of intersubjective understanding.

In another publication, Taylor (2003) comprehensively applies CCT's understanding of Gramscian hegemony to the IMF's conditionality of 'good governance'. Here he illustrates the link between 'common-sense' ideas and international institutions, and how the IMF uses 'good governance' to sustain neo-Liberalism at the world order and national levels. The conceptualisation of hegemony leans more towards 'intellectual and moral leadership' rather than the attainment of consensus by extending concessions to subordinate social forces (and states). Instead, it is argued that the IMF convinces recipient states that its programs and conditionalities are in their own interest. Here the 'ideas' side of hegemony features more strongly than the material (rewards and compromise) side. This is attributable to the fact that the topic (and the theme of the book in which Taylor's chapter appears) is the role of ideas in international organisations. It will be recalled that Cox became aware of hegemony in practice during his time at the ILO.

The national elites of recipient states are described as agents who have to deal with the IMF from within the 'passive revolution' state-society complex. They can, however, decide whether to accept or reject the conditionalities required by the IMF. The argument, nevertheless, does not deal with the intersubjective understandings of these agents, nor does it deal with social forces related to modes of production (those who bear the brunt of the costs associated with IMF structural adjustment loans). The focus of the analysis is at the world order and national levels.

Kees van der Pijl (1998) draws primarily and critically on Marx to develop his concept of 'transnational classes', but also engages (critically) with Cox to substantiate his own interpretation of forms of state. He identifies two forms, 'Lockean heartland' and 'Hobbesian contended'. These correspond to Cox's hegemonic and non-hegemonic ('passive revolution' or 'Caesarian') states. Van der Pijl adopts Cox's notion of 'state-society complex', argues that Cox's (1987) forms of state are a 'concretization' of his own classification and adds Cox's 'proto-state' concept to his two forms. There are some crucial departure points, though. Van der Pijl follows the classical Marx in focusing on the material and negating the ideational. Although he uses the concept of hegemony, it is more in a non-Gramscian sense (hegemony as dominance). Gramsci's 'passive revolution' concept is, however, used in reference to 'developing states'. Cox's important contribution is acknowledged, but criticised for being too Gramscian.

Ultimately, world order must be explained via class formation at the national level and the establishment of world dominance by the dominant class in the Lockean heartland. Changes in class relations lead (via changes in state forms) to changes at the world order level. Competing classes contest world order for their own interests, and the transnational capitalist class supports the contemporary world order. The Freemasons are regarded as an example of an institution-alised transnational class. This is not considered through the prism of CCT's hegemony and counter-hegemony. The explanation is none-theless rich in historical detail and traces the origins of capitalism to the seventeenth century. Van der Pijl also draws on art and culture to support his argument. Material capabilities are the defining feature of structures (in the Braudelian sense) and not ideas. Insti-tutions, too, emanate from the material interest of classes. They change according to the dynamics of class relations.

The above concise and selective snapshot of some of those who have been inspired by Cox's example allows us to make a number of observations. These observations are related to the point made above and in Chapter 1, viz. that the 'followers' of CCT can be divided into those who 'give a nod' to Cox – those who selectively incorporate aspects of his framework into their own explanations – and those who attempt to comprehensively apply it.

Most of the authors we considered used CCT selectively or indi-cate that Cox inspired them. The latter usually do this by emphasis-ing the link between theory and interests (in reference to the much quoted, 'theory is always *for* someone and *for* some purpose' state-ment), the equal importance which must be given to the ideational and the materialist, the non-determinist interaction between agency and structure, and the need to access the intersubjective under-standings and collective images of social forces. Stephen Gill is an interesting example because his publications are a combination of our three categorisations. In his earlier work he closely follows and incorporates Cox's conceptualisation of historical materialism and hegemony and selectively uses other aspects of CCT. Thereafter, he draws on various other sources (via his reading of Cox) to develop his own Gramscian approach to IR. Later, Cox's inspiration for the development of a 'hybrid perspective' (with Isabella Bakker) is reflected in the title of the edited volume, *Power, Production and Social Reproduction*, and in the re-interpreted incorporation of other aspects of CCT. The latter volume is notable and commendable for the contributors' focus on the dynamics of social forces at the 'fundamental social level.' Gill's long and productive association with CCT was, no doubt, facilitated by his close proximity to Cox at York University in Canada.

All of the contributions incorporate Cox's Gramscian derived conceptualisation of hegemony and consider the fit between the three components (mainly at the world order level) in terms of the concrete situations they investigate. However, the consideration of the 'fit' between ideas, institutions and material capabilities that tell us whether hegemony has been attained, is inclined to favour either ideas or material capabilities. This notwithstanding the fact that they are both regarded as equally important by the authors in our sample and that they explicitly state that both will be focused on. Alternatively, the establishment of a dominant idea is regarded as lying in the material power of the actor(s) who have a vested interest in it. The impact of ideas and material capabilities on institutions is also analysed in a determinist or linear sense. This can be attributed to the nature of the phenomenon which is being looked at, but the interaction between the ideational and materialist in the explanation of change is a cardinal component of CCT and should, therefore, be included in the analysis.

The same can be said of the relationship between structure and agency and, relatedly, the mutual influence between world orders, states and social forces (related to production). The agents that feature in CCT are collective in nature and the challenge is to determine how changes in their intersubjective understanding of their material environment impact on structural change and how structure limits their thinking and actions. Most of the contributions do not manage to engage with the impact collective agents have on structures. Social forces and the different modes of production with their associated hierarchies (for example, marginalised social forces) are, as a rule, not considered, even though they may be regarded as important. When there is an engagement at this level, the collective agents tend to conceptualised in Marxian class terms or are either national or transnational elites. A focus on contradictions (the gap between ideas and material benefits) is, generally, a theme and most authors provide (to a greater and lesser degree) some form of historical contextualisation.

From the above, we can see that the comprehensive adoption and application of CCT has been the exception. Nevertheless, the selective incorporation of his ideas would, we think, be in line with an eclecticism and a contextual reading and interpretation of his work, with which Cox himself would have no major problems. However, it should also be remembered that change, for Cox, ultimately emanates from the bottom up. How ideas (intersubjective, subjective and collective images) and material aspects interact at this level should therefore be part of the legacy that CCT presents to us. After all, as Richard Falk (1997: 53) keenly observes, the strategic-tactical dimension of CCT aims to '...achieve specificity in concrete settings of struggle between social forces aligned to the global market and those connected with more limited communities of local, national and regional scope. Cox sees the potential for the transformation of forms of state and world orders as lying within these "more limited human communities."'

The Critical Theory of Robert W. Cox: A pathway to conversations?

Cohen (2007), Dickins (2006), Phillips (2005a) and Murphy and Nelson (2001) remind us of the existence of two schools in IPE, between which, there is no or hardly any constructive dialogue. I use the word 'remind' deliberately, because the members of the mainstream (empiricist) and non-mainstream (critical/interpretive) approaches[3] seem to be so immersed in the dynamics of 'group think' that they tend to forget that there are others who follow different paths and different (productive) research agendas. They are inclined towards reading the same journals (*International Organization* and *International Studies Quarterly* for the empiricists and *New Political Economy* and *Review of International Political Economy* for the critical interpretivists) and attending the conference panels of their 'tribe' or, as Dickins (2006: 480) puts it, their 'species'. They are reminded of each other's existence when they look at introductory textbooks which list the various approaches, and/or when a member of a rival tribe wanders into a panel comprised of the 'other side' to raise the usual objections and accusations.

This state of affairs, as Cohen (2007) clearly illustrates, is not irrational. There are a number of good historical reasons that explain the divide. Space prohibits a detailed discussion of them, but it suffices to say that the division resulted in separate ontologies, epistemologies, methods, normative goals (explanation vs. justice and equity), research agendas and, crucially, the creation of distance between 'us' and 'them', as well as the inability to move out of one's comfort zone. As Cohen (2007: 200) notes, 'The process is a natural one and tends to be self-reinforcing. Once begun, its momentum is hard to overcome.' Additionally, the creation of the 'American' IPE school, which Phillips (2005a: 11) points out correctly is an intellectual rather than a geographical categorisation, was done from within the discipline of political science.[4] This means that IPE is viewed, by some, as a branch of IR, and following on from this perspective that its focus should be on issues which lie at the international or global level (finance, production, trade, governance).

Tellingly, neither of the two 'pioneers often associated with the development of the 'British IPE school' (Susan Strange and Robert Cox) were political scientists. Both favour an approach that eschews the building of grand theory, and moves from knowledge of concrete situations to explanations that draw on a variety of theories. Additionally, the development of IPE in Britain took place within the field of 'international studies' which drew on a variety of disciplines in the humanities and which was often housed in a separate department. The tendency to have a multi-disciplinary or 'cross-over' approach to explanation was thus ingrained from the beginning and the 'critical' aspect of the British version thrived in an environment were 'political economy' was not associated with Marxism or redistributive social welfare policies, as it was in the US. All of this has resulted in the current impasse that is characterised by 'mutual neglect' (Cohen, 2007: 207–15).

Some suggestions for a way forward have been made. Cohen (2007: 216–17) foresees a 'compromise' or possibly, a 'synthesis' based on the respective strengths of each approach that, if combined, can be complementary. The American school brings to the table the method of empiricism, which emphasises parsimonious theory building and hypotheses testing in order to arrive at generalisations. The British school is strong on historical contextualisation, asking questions about the underlying cause of problems, equity and justice concerns and, multi-disciplinarity.

Dickins (2006: 481–2) regards the 'differences' between the two schools as a point of departure for the initiating of a dialogue from which both sides can benefit. The time for such a dialogue, she argues, is opportune because the empiricists have been confronted by normative questions (for instance, the issue of legitimacy in global governance institutions) and the critical interpretivists have come of age. The latter no longer see their identity in 'oppositional terms', but define it in terms of the lineage of political economy and the eclecticism of multi-disciplinary diversity. Dialogue can thus be entered into from their respective positions of strength and lead to an adoption of one another's 'tools' of enquiry. Importantly, Dickins (2006: 491) ends by pointing out that a 'common vernacular' will facilitate collaboration and complementarity. For her, a 'rough but ready' vehicle for this could be the constructivist approach which focuses on 'social facts.'

Nicola Phillips (2005c: 253) suggests that the reconstruction of IPE should begin by returning to the 'idea of political economy' (see Cox, 2004: 307) and that such a project could be embarked on by both the empiricist and critical approaches. But what are the reasons for this suggestion? Phillips' (2005a: 1–7) primary concern is to argue for the 'globalizing' of IPE, which means the 'stretching' or 'expanding' of the field to cover excluded and neglected areas and issues. She contends, convincingly, that IPE has engaged predominantly with issues (trade, finance, production, governance) which are of importance to the core, industrialised states and from within their understanding and context. This has been detrimental to peripheral regions and states which are regarded as 'exceptional' and are focused on in terms of issues such as democracy, inequality, development, accountability and so on. But it has also been detrimental to a proper understanding of the core countries, because 'third world' issues are regarded as irrelevant to the study of their political economies (Phillips, 2005c: 248). To address this problem we need to think about what needs to be done to IPE itself, and not only about what needs to be included.

Phillips (2005a: 14–17) emphasises that in thinking about what needs to be done, we must consider the way in which IPE developed as a field of study. In the process of its development, the classical focus of political economy on policy, norms and dynamics without the recognition of boundaries was left behind. Contemporary IPE (both in the empiricist and critical interpretive approaches) through its association with IR (for the empiricists) focuses on the international (or the global) and leaves the national (and sub-national) levels to comparative political economy and development studies. As a result, the structural and systemic (world order) level has been prioritised, while agency and the nature of its relationship with structure has been neglected. This tendency can be clearly recognised in the work of most of the authors that we considered in the previous section.

Where agency (which I regard as a deliberate action which originates from a subject, a collective or an institution and which has detectable consequences) is incorporated, it is done so from within a core country understanding of the concept. This results in a focus on actors which are regarded as legitimate participants in a formal global, national and local 'liberal, pluralist and democratic environment.' At the global level, states, international organisations, transnational actors (banks, international financial institutions, multinational corporations) and social movements which are transnationally orientated are viewed as the primary agents (Phillips, 2005b: 47–9). So what needs to be done to IPE?

The first suggestion Phillips (2005c: 252–3) makes to move the reconstruction of IPE forward is a plea to recognise '…that what we are engaged in is, in essence, the study of *political economy*.' This requires of us a willingness to engage across disciplinary divisions (comparative political economy, development studies, social anthropology and so on) and to deploy more than one level of analysis regardless of whether we are focusing on a local, national, regional, or global concrete issue. She hastens to add that this does not mean that IPE should be made redundant or that analysts should no longer focus on its traditional core issues, but that the lines of demarcation should be blurred. In doing so, she stops short of Cox's (2002: 79–80) conclusion that IR and IPE have become obsolete, because 'In so far as we begin to see social relations as the foundation of political authorities and the origin of conflicts, the conventional separation of comparative politics from international relations makes little sense.' The reality of an institutionalised IPE (with its own journals, books, career paths, conference panels and so on), however, signals that these observations are really more related to how we should change our thinking, than to a practical course of action.

The second suggestion relates to the relationship between structure and agency as well as agents that have been neglected. Phillips (2005c: 254–6) proposes a perspective that recognises that structure and agency are 'mutually constitutive' of one another. Additionally, the focus should not be limited to agents who operate in formal, 'legitimate' environments but also on marginalised actors who participate in informal settings. Therefore, the particular context (political economy) within which agents interact with structures becomes extremely important, so as to identify the limitations which are unique to a specific setting, as well as the ability of agents to have an impact on them. Finally, power should be understood in structural, material and ideational terms, and IPE should incorporate development (understood in non-linear terms and as something which happens in all countries) as a 'central organizing concept' (Phillips, 2005c: 261, 266).

I propose that CCT is the vehicle that, in a somewhat adapted form, can move us forward to address the suggestions and concerns of Cohen, Dickins and Phillips. The first important point which needs to be made in terms of CCT being a pathway to a conversation on methodology and ontology between empiricists and critical interpretivists is that it has made no claim to being post-positivist, post-Westphalian (in the sense that states are regarded as an endangered species, to continue with Dickins' metaphor), or anti-foundationalist. Notwithstanding the fact that it is often associated with the small 'c' critical approaches in IR (because it points to the limitations of problem-solving theory) it does not reject positivism as fundamentally flawed from the outset and therefore not salvageable.

Here, I think, Phillips (2005b: 28–9) goes too far when she implies that Cox's distinction between critical and problem-solving theory can be directly and sympathetically linked to the post-positivist debate in critical IPE. The point on problem-solving (positivist empiricism) that Cox regards as 'useful within its limits' was argued and substantiated in Chapter 1, and will not be repeated here. However, he points out that its utility (to provide a synchronic 'snapshot') diminishes in times of significant change because it works optimally under stable (*status quo*) conditions. To identify the contradictions (of which the problems are symptoms) in historical structures and explain change within them requires the 'historical diachronic approach' (personal communication, 6 April 2007). A combination of the two methods should, therefore, be possible, as long as the results of the problem-solving method are located within a diachronic analysis of prevailing historical structures and historically contextualised. Admittedly, this will be a challenging task, but it will be made easier by cross-disciplinary and inter-disciplinary collaboration, as well as an acceptance that the concrete situation should determine the method and not the other way around. Such a project would result in empiricism of the critical kind, or alternatively, critical empiricism.

I differ from Cohen's (2007: 211) observation on Cox, that it '...is difficult to convert his conclusions into empirically falsifiable propositions.' Cox's (1987, 1999a) detailed conceptualisation of twelve modes of production (most of them still relevant) and his description of a hierarchy (integrated, precarious and marginalised) in terms of which social forces are related to the contemporary world political economic order can usefully be applied to concrete situations in order to 'operationalise' someone's economic position. Furthermore, Cox (see for instance, 1981, 1987, 1993b, 1997b) has consistently pointed out that marginalised social forces (subsistence farmers, street hawkers, vendors, casual unskilled labourers) are a *potential* source of instability and change because they derive no, or very little benefits from the dominant globally orientated mode of production. He has qualified this by noting that this potential is 'diffused' because the efforts of the marginalised '... are directed to personal and family survival rather than protest' (Cox, 2002: 84).

These are claims that can be investigated using a variety of methods (focus group analysis, unstructured or structured interviews, survey analysis) in order to ascertain whether the attributes that we postulate are characteristic of marginalised social forces can be empirically substantiated (see Leysens, 2006).[5] A critical empiricist perspective, however, must be sensitive to the fact that these methods result in 'snapshots' and are imperfect instruments. For instance, survey research can, without the necessary precautions, present a distorted picture of the aggregated attitudes that are being fathomed. Moreover, the idea that this particular instrument of empiricist research is more valuable (to practitioners and academics) because it is more accurate and precise is a hazardous one and should be debunked. The recent construction of a number of global indexes (the corruption index, freedom house index, transformation index, globalisation index, the world value index, and various regional 'barometers'), though useful within limits, should be subjected to critical analysis and treated with caution. They are often presented in the form of ahistorical and uncontextualised 'snapshots' which decision-makers then use to grant or hold back investment funds, loans and aid, as well as to assess which countries are market friendly and committed to liberal democracy. Comparing countries in this way also contributes to the idea and the formation of the 'competition' state.

The state, as we have seen, remains an important institution/ agent in CCT. Regardless of the fact that its autonomy has been eroded and that it has had to adapt to an environment where there are multiple centres of authority, Cox (2002, 2004) views the state as both the problem and the solution. This should re-assure those empiricists in IR/IPE who regard the critical interpretative school as dismissive of the state as agent and institution. There are a number of other attributes of CCT that are conducive to the initiation of a dialogue and a reconstruction of IPE along the lines that Phillips suggests.

Negotiations between uncompromising adversaries are often brokered and mediated by a third party. Cox is an 'outsider' in the sense that he has contributed to the fields of IR/IPE without having followed the normal academic route to them. He is primarily a historian and approaches political economy from a historian's perspective. This poses a substantial challenge to IR/IPE scholars who want to apply the historical method that lies at the core of CCT. I will return to this point below. The advantage of being an outsider is that one is not subjected to the 'group-think' of a tribe that, by its very nature, is intent on keeping its members within the fold. It also results in a greater willingness to adopt an eclectic approach to the use of theory and to cross artificial borders. Cox (2002: 80) emphasises that it is '…necessary to breach sacrosanct disciplinary boundaries so as to draw upon history and sociology and geography – indeed upon all the social sciences and humanities'. This is fundamental to the idea of political economy.

Another strong point of CCT is its multi-level approach, that also allows for a regional point of entry; 'For the purpose of understanding

world order or regional development, it is necessary to draw together knowledge about power relations in society and knowledge
about relations among the entities like states which are shaped by
those power relations.' (Cox, 2002: 80). Fundamental social relations are regarded as preceding international relations; they are 'the
foundation of political authorities and the origin of conflicts'. It will
be recalled that Cox (1981: 147) also emphasises that challenges to
world order hegemony must start through the 'long, laborious effort to
build new historic blocs within national boundaries'. These premises
of CCT, together with its emphasis on the role of contemporary
marginalised social forces and 'limited human communities', mean
that (a) the analyst starts by looking at the local and thereafter moves
outwards to make the transnational connections to the global, and
(b) the focus is not only on 'legitimate' participation within the formal
institutionalised setting of state-society relations or global civil society.
This addresses the problems of 'neglect' and the privileging of the
'international' in IPE.

The historical method[6] of CCT unambiguously conceptualises
agency and structure as being 'mutually constitutive'. Structures act
as constraints on human action, but it is (collective) human action
and understandings which creates them and, ultimately changes
them. Additionally, a unity between subject (shared understandings,
collective images) and object (institutions and social practices) is
assumed. Institutions are the result of collective human responses to
their environment and change (or the potential for it) can therefore
be explained through an understanding of the intersubjective ideas
that people have acquired with respect to their institutions and
practices. Cox's understanding of agency (subject) focuses on the
collective rather than the individual, and requires a rethinking of
the thoughts of past actors. Over the longer term, subjects develop
certain mental images (the Braudelian concept of *mentalité*) in relation to their material environment and the institutions (a structural
outcome) that result from their collective interactions. According
to Cox, accessing or 'reconstituting' these intersubjective understandings (for which there is no 'formula'), 'is the essence of an historian's task and the most complex part of it' (personal communication,
15 November 2007).

It is this reconstructing or 'recapturing' of past (and present) intersubjective understandings[7] which has proven to be the greatest

challenge to those political economists who want to incorporate a focus on contemporary social forces, as well as those who have not managed to move beyond the international level. I propose that the way forward is through an engagement with social anthropology and development studies, both of which are interested in explaining the political economy of marginalised social forces at the local level and how they interact with their immediate material and ideational environment. From there, one can move 'outwards' (and back inwards) to incorporate and explain the state-society complex and world order.[8] In this way, but primarily through the legacy of Robert Cox's contribution as a 'lone' outsider, the promise of a critical (empiricist) (I)PE may still be fulfilled. Nevertheless, I think that the legacy of being a 'fugitive' rather than being regarded and remembered as a guru, is the one that Cox would prefer. After all, as he remarked about Susan Strange's work which was not absorbed into mainstream American IR/IPE but inspired many students on both sides of the Atlantic and further a field, 'This relative neglect must be taken as a badge of honour rather than a failing.' (Cox, 1999c: 14). Regardless of what happens to the idea of political economy, the same, I think, will be said about the work of Robert W. Cox.

Notes

Chapter 1   Why a Book on the Critical Theory of Robert W. Cox?

1   My point of departure is that IPE, later Global Political Economy (GPE), is the more encompassing field of study, because to some extent it has encouraged multi-disciplinary inputs, critical historical thinking about the nature of social change, and a sensitivity to the contextualisation of theory (Cox, 2002: 79–80). It has also broadened our understanding of the dynamic interaction between politics and economics from a wide variety of perspectives. The need to accept this as a starting premise was famously made by Susan Strange (1970) in a seminal article. I derive my understanding and ontology of IPE and its recent companion, GPE, from Cox's (1999a: 11–12) conceptualisation of the 'global economy.'

    Drawing on Madeuf and Michalet's (1978) distinction between the international economy and a (then emerging) more integrated form, he notes that in contemporary terms 'global economy' refers to the two driving forces behind economic globalisation. These are the organisation of production and finance on a level, which transcends the traditional boundaries between states. Co-existing with the global economy is the international economy. The latter consists of traditional inter-state trade and sections of the domestic economy that are disconnected from the global economy, but are nevertheless constrained by it. Together they form, what Cox calls, the 'world economy.' Global Political Economy can be distinguished from IPE in that it incorporates a focus on economic globalisation's affect on 'power relations among social forces and states', its supportive institutions, and on forms of resistance (Cox, 1999a: 12). I would add that GPE also attempts to explain why and how some states and social forces adapt and accommodate to economic globalisation.

    Later, Cox (2002: 79–80) suggests that the fields of IR/IPE have become obsolete. He argues for a 'more integrated form of knowledge' which draws on 'all the social sciences and humanities' to understand world order, states and how both are shaped by fundamental social relations. Considering that critical IPE has not managed to bridge the distance between intellectuals concerned with social equity and those who are marginalised so as to enhance our understanding at the local level (Murphy, 2007), I empathise with Cox's observation.

2   See for instance, Murphy (2007) and Cox's address to the University of Sheffield's Political Economy Research Centre on the occasion of its 10th anniversary in 2003. The text of the address was published in the journal, *New Political Economy* (Cox, 2004).

3   Cox's experience at the International Labour Organisation (ILO) had a lasting influence on his view of international organisations. Their potential

to act as channels for counter-hegemonic challenges '…can be ruled out as a total illusion' (Cox, 1983: 139). Later, he participated in the United Nations University (UNU) Multilateralism in the UN System (MUNS) project. This resulted in an edited volume (Cox, 1997a), which argued for a 'new realism' (more inclusive and 'structural-critical') approach to multilateralism. Nevertheless, he reiterates his scepticism in 'reflections and transitions' when he foresees the UN as a 'site' where issues can be raised to heighten awareness over the long run, but from where the momentum for 'structural change' is unlikely to originate (Cox, 2002: 40).

4   Later, Cox (1999a: 12) pointed out that the regional level is another important analytical layer that can be incorporated, together with the local level.

5   Although Cox consistently emphasises the potential of those social forces who are marginalised or excluded from the global economy he is careful to point out that being marginalised is in itself not a sufficient condition to bring about transformation. Rather, increasing inequality creates the 'systemic' potential for instability. This, if the marginalised were effectively mobilised, could result in a populist backlash and/or proactive countermeasures by the state. The marginalised are, however, difficult to organise because they are concerned with daily survival strategies. However, this does not mean that they are not involved in poverty reduction strategies through local projects and networks (Cox, 1987: 387–91, Cox, 1999a: 11 and personal communication with the author, 31 March 2007).

6   Production is and remains a starting point for CCT, but in a non-reductionist and non-determinist sense. Reflecting on his critics and the development of his own thinking, Cox (2002: 31) notes: 'What began for me as a study of existing organisation for the production of goods and services became conceptually expanded to include the production of institutions, law, morality and ideas.'

7   The reason for this can be found in Cox's diverse intellectual roots and the eclectic incorporation of these into his thinking. In his own words, 'I do not shy away from the word "eclectic."' (Cox, 2002: 29).

8   Cox (1986: 248–9), in a postscript to 'Social Forces, States and World Orders: Beyond International Relations Theory', admits to being a historical materialist and to finding the work of the historical (not the 'determinist') Marx useful. Later, in 'Reflections and transitions', he confirms his eclectic use of Marx (his critics regard this as an unacceptable dilution of the pure form), 'I have no pretensions to the title of Marxist, though I admire many scholars who legitimately have that title.' (Cox, 2002: 28). This has not prevented the confusion and the subsequent 'tagging'. Chinese university students who have been exposed to PPWO (which was recently translated into Chinese) regard Cox as a neo-Marxist! (personal communication, 31 March 2007). Others have concluded that he is a '…a fairly conventional Marxist (Marxist-Leninist even)…' (Brown, 1992: 202). Burnham (1999: 39; 1991: 89), who is regarded by Cox as a 'seriously committed Marxist' (personal communication, 31 March 2007), on the other hand, criticises Cox for his Weberian 'methodological pluralism' and his 'Gramscian inspired view' that the state has an autonomous role to play

vis-à-vis capital, labour and accumulation (in other words, production relations). Cox notes that he (Burnham) is '…quite right to point out that I am not a proper Marxist. At the same time, anti-Marxists will sniff Marxism in my work and exclude it from consideration for that reason' (personal communication, 31 March 2007).

9   I will return to the neo-Gramscian categorisation in Chapter 6, when I discuss the followers of CCT.

10   Capitals (CT) are used to indicate the association with the Frankfurt School and to distinguish CT from criticism in the study of literature, as well as to distinguish it from post-modernist approaches in IR (Morrow with Brown, 1994: 14, 32). The need to make the distinction between CT and post-modernism as critical approaches in IR is correctly pointed out by Brown (1994: 214): 'It is not possible to be a Critical Theorist and a post-modernist – although, using my initial definition, post-modernists are critical theorists.' As will be indicated below both approaches are 'critical' (lower case) in the sense that they are disillusioned with the dominant (modernist) approach to knowledge creation. For CT, however, bearing in mind the need to be 'reflexive' about theory, the modernist project can be reconstructed. Post-modernists regard the foundations of Enlightenment rationality as fundamentally unsound from the outset.

11   Cox points out explicitly that his association with the Frankfurt School is 'non-existent'. He admits to having read and appreciated Habermas' *Legitimation Crisis*, but does not regard himself as a serious student of Habermas' work or as knowledgeable on the contributions of any of the other authors associated with the Frankfurt School (personal communication, 31 March 2007). This observation is corroborated by the 'genealogical' review I undertook of his work and citations.

12   See also Dickins (2006). I have read the mini-debate in *RIPE*, 15(1) February 2008 which resulted from Cohen's (2007) article. At the time, the book manuscript was already with the publishers, being processed in proof form. I cannot elaborate in more detail here, but remain convinced that Cohen's distinction is useful and that being afloat in 'mid-Atlantic' is, perhaps, not a bad place to be.

13   The point is not original. Germain (1999), in a review essay of three books on European Monetary Union (EMU), distinguishes between the 'outside account' (empiricist) and the 'inside account' (context sensitive, interpretive) as two types of explanation in IPE. These can both contribute to explanation individually, but would be more effective if combined by '…nesting the narrow view into its broader and more historical or sociological cousin' (Germain, 1999: 391). He adds that this would be a 'daunting task'.

14   When asked to indicate whether the interview with Germain still reflected his thinking on the problem-solving/critical theory distinction, Cox replied in the affirmative. He also emphasised that this distinction is related to the synchronic and diachronic approach. The former focusing on a 'snapshot of reality' that assumes systemic stability and the latter concerned with explaining structural change (personal communication, 6 April 2007).

Chapter 2   Influences, Context, and Theoretical Development

1   Motivating his interest in the concept of civilisations, he notes 'The attempt to recover the sense of spirit behind the historical is what motivates me to explore the idea of civilisations.' (Cox, 1999b: 392).

2   To illustrate this point he refers to the domestic support that David Morse mustered in the United States (for example, the American Federation of Labor-Congress of Industrial Organisations, AFL-CIO) to counter the possibility of the US pulling out of the ILO, after the Soviet Union re-entered the organisation in 1954. The support was forthcoming because Morse's policies carried the approval of the AFL-CIO, in the sense that they were perceived as being anti-Communist. Later, when Morse came under pressure to appoint someone from the Soviet Union as assistant director-general, the support was withdrawn. Shortly thereafter, Morse resigned (Cox, 1969: 339, editors note, Cox with Sinclair, 1996: 340).

3   Cox (1976: 178–9) distinguishes between data and facts to emphasise the difference between the positivist and 'other approaches.' Data, as defined by positivism, are measurable objects (even mental attitudes can be measured, as in survey research, he notes). Facts (historical events), in contrast, can be understood by humans because humans have made them. Drawing on Giambattista Vico via Collingwood, Cox, notes that understanding is only possible if the event has been made by the knower (a human product) (footnote 8, p. 179).

4   In later publications, Cox explains that this is not a form of idealism (the external world being a mere creation of the human mind). He motivates the connection between consciousness and being by citing Collingwood (Cox, 1976: 181–2, footnote, 12). In the quotation, Collingwood stresses the distinction between 'the outside and inside of an event.' The outside, for him, is historical events observable as acts of behaviour. The inside, 'can only be described in terms of thought'. What Collingwood means is that an event can only be understood by linking it to the thought of the agent who is involved in it: action is the unity of the outside and inside of an event...'

5   In the 1981 article, Cox's (1981: 98) 'coherent structural arrangement' becomes 'historical structure.' Also, in that article, 'behaviour patterns' changes to 'capabilities' The capabilities which Cox refers to are related to material conditions: productive capacity, destructive capacity (military), natural resources, technology, industry and wealth (economic growth/ development). The change from 'behaviour patterns' to 'capabilities' is probably motivated by the need to connect the notion of a 'historical structure' to the assumption that collective actions of humans and their resultant organisations are the result of their response to the material challenges of their existence.

6   The long absence had a lasting impact on Cox, as reflected in the proposed title of his memoirs, 'Universal foreigner. A Canadian Life' (personal communication, 31 March 2007).

7   See also Cox (1982: 39) 'Ultimately, all forms of power...depend upon control over production...'

8 Cox (1981) would later (sympathetically) criticise Wallerstein's world systems theory as inadequate because he does not think it accounts for systemic change (see Chapter 3).

Chapter 3   The Core Theoretical Framework and Beyond

1 Cox (1981: 116–17) motivates his use of the concept 'world order' in a footnote (nr 2). He prefers it to 'inter-state system' because it can be applied to periods during which the modern state did not yet exist (e.g. medieval Europe). It also avoids the universal connotations and continuity associated with the concept 'system.' The term 'world' is used because it refers to a 'designated totality, geographically limited by the range of probable interactions.' The term 'order' does not discount instability, but is used to refer to patterns. The plural form, 'orders', refers to characteristics, which endure over time and (comparatively) allow us to distinguish between different world orders.

2 The need for critical theory to concern itself with practice and strategy, rather than an idealist type end-goal is, again, stressed in PPWO (1987): 'Critical understanding focuses on…the possibilities of launching a social movement rather than on what the movement might achieve', this '…must be distinguished from utopian thinking' (Cox, 1987: 393). Cox's own perspective on social equity is derived from the conservatism espoused by Edmund Burke, who had a 'organic and solidaristic vision of society.' In other words a sense of community above individual interest. He is quick to point out, though, that he does not want to be associated with 'those who have appropriated it (conservatism) to cloak an egoistic defence of acquired privilege.' (Cox, 1979: 416, footnote 1). His conservatism is 'more consistent with socialism than with the possessive individualism of economic liberalism' (Cox, 1996b: 20). This alternative vision, which is to be arrived at through strategic practice and critical analysis, is one, which involves a shift away from consumerism and excessive individualism (Cox, 1987: 402).

3 The historical structures approach differs from structuralism in that 'structures are made by collective human action and transformable by collective human action' (Cox, 1987: 395). The transformation of structures is possible because there is a shared intersubjective understanding between individuals, which extends to abstract concepts such as the state. The state exists because 'In being so shared, these ideas constitute the social world of these same individuals.' Therefore, although, humans are mostly 'born into' existing structures, the latter are not immutable, but have been created and can therefore be changed. In this way historical structures are a component of people's material world (Cox, 1987: 395).

4 Cox maintained this scepticism regarding the potential role of international organisations to facilitate a counter-hegemonic challenge. See for instance the following comment: 'Therefore, the key to future world order is to be sought, not so much in the sphere of international institutions or 'regimes', as in the political leadership that may be able to

consolidate a socio-political base from the mutations now going on in production' (Cox, 1989b: 49). See also the interview with Randall Germain (1999b) and Cox (2002).

5   The dynamic interaction between social forces, forms of state and world orders is described in rich historical detail in PPWO (1987), and is related to three historical structures; *pax brittanica*, rival imperialisms, and *pax americana*. For instance, the rise and incorporation of the industrial working class in England (social forces) led to a new form of state; welfarist-nationalist. This change in the form of state led to a world order, which was characterised by increased rivalry (military and industrial), between the major European powers. World orders also influence forms of state. The bipolar order, a characteristic of the Cold War, contributed to the rise of the military industrial complex in the former Union of Soviet Socialist Republics (USSR) and the USA. Forms of state (based on the interests of the dominant social forces) influence the power relations between contending social forces related to production (Cox, 1981: 100–1).

To extend the example, the interaction between ideas, material capabilities and institutions, as well as the relations between social forces, forms of state, and world orders can be illustrated by the historical structure of the *pax brittanica*. The liberal form of state in nineteenth century England was founded upon the attainment of middle class hegemony. The 1832 Reform Act gave the middle class representation in parliament and excluded the working class, thereby thwarting attempts to create an alliance between the two. In 1846, the repeal of the Corn Laws signalled the triumph of industrial over agrarian interests. The functions of the liberal state were centred on the creation of an unregulated economy. A 'pure' labour market was created (based on supply and demand), poverty became a personal responsibility (1834 Poor Law Reform), and employers-worker relations were based on bipartism. The ideas (ideology) underpinning the liberal state form were based on the separation between politics and economics (*laissez-faire*). Ironically, de-regulation of the market, was accompanied by growing centralisation and bureaucratisation of state power.

At the world order level, hegemony was maintained by England's capacity (military and maritime domination) to manage the balance of power in Europe. The same capacity was also used to assure freedom of commercial access and an open trade order. Although there were no institutions comparable to the IMF and World Bank (created at the outset of the *pax americana*), the City of London was responsible for maintaining a gold exchangeable currency (the gold standard). The contradictions in the liberal state form arose from the social costs (unemployment, poverty, starvation, child labour, appalling work conditions) that accompanied the functioning of the unregulated market. Pressure by organised labour and sympathetic industrialists (e.g. Chamberlain) led to the promulgation of social safety net laws and the re-embedding of the market into society (Cox, 1987: 123–47).

6   I find Scholte's (2005) conceptualisation of globalisation useful and distinct. He regards the multifaceted process of globalisation as different

from previous epochs, because the essence of the process is 'deterritorial-isation.' This means that we can only understand the dynamics associated with it by using the globe as a unit of analysis. In doing this, distance and time become irrelevant. For instance, in the cases of global finance and global production.

7 Later, Cox (1992a: 298–9, 301) introduced the concept 'nébuleuse' to explain the aftermath of the changes that took place in the Bretton Woods order during 1968–1975. It refers to the ascendancy of global finance and its increasing autonomy from global production. The removal of national capital control regulations, initiated by the US, resulted in states becoming 'accountable to external bond markets and global financial interests', a form of 'governance without government.'

8 Or, as stated in the interview with Randall Germain, 'Reality is a response by people to problems they confront and by the way they understand them and deal with them' (Cox, 1999b: 393).

9 The following quotations and excerpts are indicative of the importance, which Cox attaches to this requirement. Referring to the need for the historian to 'think himself into (an) action', Cox (1976: 182, footnote 12) stresses that the (historian's) 'main task' is to 'discern the thought' of the agent who committed it. In 'Labor and Hegemony' he emphasises the importance of reconstructing the mental frameworks through which individuals and groups perceive their action (Cox, 1980: 475). Finally, 'The mind is the privileged channel of access to understanding how social institutions are constructed to cope with material problems...' (Cox, 1996b: 28).

Chapter 4   The Critical Theory of the Frankfurt School

1 Ashley (1981), in a seminal article, was among the first to argue for the incorporation of CT into IR, when he attempted to link Habermas' notion of knowledge-constitutive interests to what he described as 'practical' and 'technical' realism. However, he subsequently rejected CT as foundationalist and his later work saw a move towards post-modernism (Haacke, 1996: 271 and Keyman, 1997: 100). This point will be elaborated on in Chapter 5.

2 Kellner (1989: 1) notes that referring to those associated with the Institute as the 'Frankfurt School' ignores the fact that much of the work done by what he sees as the major figures was done during their years of exile in the United States. He also emphasises that there were as many differences as there were similarities.

3 Other names which Held (1980: 14) associates with the Institute as a whole are: Franz Neumann, Otto Kirchheimer, Henryk Grossman, Arkadij Gurland, and on the 'outer circle', Walter Benjamin.

4 Technically, Karl Albert Gerlach preceded Grünberg, but he was unable to take up the directorship because of his premature death (Kellner, 1989: 13).

5   One of the first projects initiated during Horkheimer's time as director was a quantitative survey of white and blue collar German workers. Headed by Erich Fromm (who was assisted by Paul Lazarsfeld and Hilde Weiss), the publication of the results were delayed because of differences in opinion (related to methodological and theoretical problems) over their usefulness and the going into exile of the Institute members. A final (incomplete) publication, *Arbeiter und Angestellte am Vorabend des Dritten Reiches*, appeared in 1980. The translated version is: Erich Fromm. 1984. *The Working Class in Weimar Germany*. Cambridge, Mass.: Harvard University Press (Kellner, 1989: 20, 237, footnote 33 and Morrow with Brown, 1994: 104).

6   Between 1939 and 1941 it was published in English as *Studies in Philosophy and Social Science*, after which it was discontinued due to the financial difficulties experienced by the Institute (Held, 1980: 34, 37).

7   Erich Fromm, a psychoanalyst, published his key theoretical views on Marx, Freud and social psychology in 1932, the year before the Institute went into exile. They appeared in the *Journal of Social Research* and were later translated as, *The Crisis of Psychoanalysis: Essays on Freud, Marx and Social Psychology*. Greenwich, Conn: Fawcett Publications (1971) (Held, 1980: 488).

8   Both Kellner (1989) and Held (1980) point out that, although Habermas showed an initial interest in praxis by virtue of his early work on radical democracy, he later became critical of the 1960s student movement. He pointed out that while they espoused democratic goals, they were essentially following an agenda that implied a move towards censure. As a result he began to focus more on theory during the 1970s, a trend that continued after he returned to the Institute in the early 1980s (Kellner, 1989: 206, 211–12 and Held, 1980: 250–1).

9   Cox observes that he does not object to the term, 'emancipatory', but that he does not use it himself (personal communication, 31 March 2007).

10   According to Adorno and Horkheimer in *Dialectics of Enlightenment* (1947), the notion of science (instrumental reason) as a form of domination and control over nature and humans is the legacy of the Enlightenment.

11   A good account of Critical Theory's critique of positivism can be found in Marcuse (1941), where he evaluates the rise of 'positive philosophy' by looking at, among others, August Comte (Marcuse, 1941: 340–60).

12   Held's (1980: 163–4) reading of Adorno's and Horkheimer's texts suggests that their view of positivism is based on five premises: (1) all knowledge must be attributable to 'sense' experience (2) observation is the base of meaning (3) concepts can be 'operationalised', they represent/correspond to reality (4) knowledge creation must be based on one unified view of science, aiming at explanation and predictability according to the deductive-nomological model (5) facts and values must be separated.

13   This point (as related by Held, 1980: 169–70) is also made by Adorno, and Adorno and Horkheimer in *Dialectic of Enlightenment*. Positivist

science critiques other more 'ideological' approaches that are value-laden, but negates the inherent values in its own view of science: rationality and parsimony in using the best 'technical' means to achieve a stated end. In the words of Adorno (quoted in Held, 1980: 169–71): 'Value and value freedom are not separate; rather, they are contained in one another.'

Chapter 5   The 'Critical Turn' in International Relations

1   Murphy (2007) uses the term 'critical turn' in an article which 'takes stock' of the achievements and shortcomings of CT in IR. He regards Cox, but more so Ashley, as initiators of a critical school in IR, the members of which would later be called 'dissidents' by Ashley and Walker (1990a).

2   Linklater uses Bernstein, Habermas and Ashley to posit an epistemological difference between positivism, phenomenology, and critical theory. These approaches to knowledge are linked in his 1990 volume to three perspectives in IR.

3   His treatment of Cox's work, here, is less critical and he holds the latter up as an example of CT in IR, against Waltz's neo-Realism (Linklater, 1992: 86–7).

4   Keyman (1997) in an attempt to develop a 'critical social theory of international relations' from a post-colonial critical perspective also deals with issues of exclusion and inclusion. He is particularly concerned with how 'the critical turn helps us to break with the practice of inclusion/exclusion with which international relations theory operates' (Keyman, 1997: 99). Keyman finds that the various strands of CT in IR (according to him, Habermas, Cox and Linklater) tend to ignore the voice of the excluded or the 'other'. He posits that '…any critical theory of international relations cannot afford *not* to learn from the Other, *not* to reconstruct itself on the basis of the questions that the Other poses, and *not* to think of identity/difference from the lenses of the Other' (Keyman, 1997: 146). Referring to Linklater's CT of IR, he points to '…the concealed patriarchal and Eurocentric tendency…' (Keyman, 1997: 109).

5   A notable exception is the excellent edited volume by Bakker and Gill (2003a) who offer a reinterpretation of CCT and use its insights so as to incorporate marginalised social forces. This 'hybridized new intellectual space' is interdisciplinary and brings in a focus on how social reproduction is related to production and power (see Chapter 6).

6   References to 'The Poverty of Neorealism' article, which originally appeared in *International Organization*, 1984, 38 (2): 225–86, come from the edited reprint in Keohane (ed.) 1986. *Neorealism and Its Critics*.

7   By foundationalist, post-modernists mean the resorting to, or falling back on, the foundations of scientific enquiry. See for instance John Vasquez's (1995: 230) list of criteria for good theories in IR: '…accurate,

falsifiable, capable of evincing great explanatory power, progressive as opposed to degenerating in terms of their research programme(s), consistent with what is known in other areas, appropriately parsimonious and elegant'. This notion of foundationalism is taken back to the Enlightenment that is criticised by post-modernists for its belief in progress (an end goal attainable by making use of science and rationality) and for its assumption that there is an end-goal (modernity, human perfection or for that matter the ultimate realisation of human potential) (Vasquez, 1995: 219).

8   See for instance Biersteker (1989), Holsti (1989), Lapid (1989a, 1989b), and George (1989).

9   Mainly the work of Ashley (1987, 1988), Ashley and Walker (1990) and Walker (1988, 1989 and 1993).

10   See Nicholson (quoted in Neufeld, 1995: 105): 'the firmer is our knowledge of social behaviour, the greater our potential control over it.'

Chapter 6   The Legacy of Coxian Critical Theory

1   Reflecting on what the fundamental difference could be between his own approach and the Frankfurt School/CT in IR authors, Cox notes that 'My aversion to the word "emancipatory" might be the clue'. He observes that he does not share the 'optimism' associated with the Enlightenment and its descendents, but belongs to a more 'pessimistic' subterranean anti-Enlightenment tradition which is more aware of the 'constraints of history' and the 'fallibility of human nature'. In this sense he regards himself as a 'conservative in the classic Aristotelian and even Confucian idea of the organic nature of society'. This conservatism is consistent with the social democratic ideal of an interventionist state which protects the marginalised in society (personal communication, December 2007).

2   I am indebted and grateful to Audun Solli (a graduate student at the Department of Political Science, University of Stellenbosch) for the research and analysis he undertook to make the inclusion of this section possible.

3   Dickins (2006: 480) elaborating on the 'species' image refers to the two approaches as *Ratiosaurus* and *Querimonia*.

4   Cohen (2007: 206–7) points to the irony of the 'creeping economism' in the American IPE school which has brought about a swing towards 'number-crunching' techniques and the reductionist, inclusive theories of neo-classical Economics.

5   For instance, marginalised social forces in South Africa have recently engaged in collective violent acts to protest lack of service delivery and housing in informal settlements.

6   Randall Germain (2005: 8–17), in an unpublished paper, provides us with a very useful elaboration and explanation of the historical method (or 'historical mode of thought'), by engaging directly with the sources (Collingwood, Carr and Braudel) that have influenced Cox's thinking on this.

7 An excellent example of an attempt to access an individual's subjective understanding of war and occupation is Hill's (1999) account of the experiences of a French soldier (Gustave Folcher) during World War II.
8 A good example is the work being done by the Development Research Centre's (DRC, at the Institute of Development Studies, University of Sussex) project on Citizenship, Participation and Accountability. This project (now in its eighth year) focuses on the opportunities for participation by marginalised citizens in seven countries. A South African social anthropologist, Steven Robbins, is engaged in preliminary research on the political economy of housing and land, with a focus on current events that are unfolding in a marginalised, informal settlement community in Langa, Cape Town. The South African state has embarked on a national project to abolish slums and, as a result, the people of the community in question are to be relocated elsewhere because they will not be able to afford the rental and bonded houses that will be constructed on the land they are occupying.

   Moreover, the developer is a black economic empowerment company that supports the idea of market-driven provision of housing. Two national social movements (the Anti-Eviction Campaign and Abahlali baseMjondolo) are helping people to resist the resettlement. Robbins perceptively connects the problem of 'good intentions' which are not appreciated to the nature of the South African state, which he describes as 'modernist' and has a specific 'vision' of development and the market. Robbins, concludes that 'Things can only change if the residents win their court case against the removal…or the state decides to abandon this particular model of market-driven housing development…' (DRC e-conference, 19 November 2007). This example readily lends itself for 'outward movement'. First, to the nature of the South African state and how it approximates the idea of the 'competition' state. Then to a locating of the South African state into the contemporary world order.

   See also, the edited volume, *Participatory Governance? Citizens and the State in South Africa*, by Thompson (2007).

Bibliography

Adorno, T. and Horkheimer, M. 1979 (first published in 1944) *Dialectic of Enlightenment*. London: Verso.

Aronowitz, S. 1972 'Introduction', in Horkheimer, M. (translated by O'Connell, M.J. and others) *Critical Theory: Selected Essays*. New York: The Seabury Press.

Ashley, R.K. 1981 'Political Realism and Human Interests', *International Studies Quarterly*, 25 (2): 204–36.

Ashley, R.K. 1986 'The Poverty of Neorealism', in R.O. Keohane (ed.) *Neorealism and its Critics*. New York: Columbia University Press.

Ashley, R.K. 1987 'The Geopolitics of Geopolitical Space: Towards a Critical Social Theory of International Politics', *Alternatives*, 12: 404–34.

Ashley, R.K. 1988 'Untying the Sovereign State: A Double Reading of the Anarchy Problematique', *Millennium: Journal of International Studies*, 17: 227–62.

Ashley, R.K. and Walker, R.B.J. 1990 'Speaking the Language of Exile: Dissident Thought in International Studies', *International Studies Quarterly*, 34 (3): 259–68.

Bakker, I. and Gill, S. (eds) 2003a *Power, Production and Social Reproduction*. Houndmills, Basingstoke, Hampshire: Palgrave Macmillan.

Bakker, I. and Gill, S. 2003b 'Global Political Economy and Social Reproduction', in Bakker, I. and Gill, S. (eds) *Power, Production and Social Reproduction*. Houndmills, Basingstoke, Hampshire: Palgrave Macmillan.

Bakker, I. and Gill, S. 2003c 'Ontology, Method, and Hypotheses', in Bakker, I. and Gill, S. (eds) *Power, Production and Social Reproduction*. Houndmills, Basingstoke, Hampshire: Palgrave Macmillan.

Banks, M. 1985 'The Inter-Paradigm Debate', in M. Light and A.J.R. Groom (eds) *International Relations: A Handbook of Current Theory*. London: Frances Pinter.

Baylis, J. and Smith, S. (eds) 2001 *The Globalization of World Politics: An Introduction to International Relations (2nd edition)*. Oxford: Oxford University Press.

Bergin, T.G. and Fisch, M.H. 1970 *The New Science of Giambattista Vico*. Ithaca: Cornell University Press.

Bernstein, R. 1976 *The Restructuring of Social and Political Theory*. Oxford: Basil Blackwell.

Bieler, A. 1998 'Austria's Application to the European Community: a neo-Gramscian case-study of European integration', *New Political Economy*, 3 (1): 27–44.

Bieler, A. 2000 *Globalisation and Enlargement of the EU: Austrian and Swedish social forces in the struggle over membership*. London: Routledge.

Bieler, A. 2002 'The Struggle over EU Enlargement: A Historical Materialist Analysis of European Integration', *Journal of European Public Policy*, 9 (4): 575–97.

Bieler, A. and Morton, A.D. 2001 'The Gordian Knot of Agency-Structure in IR: A Neo-Gramscian Perspective', *European Journal of International Relations*, 7 (1): 5–35.

Bieler, A. and Morton, A.D. 2004 'A Critical Theory route to Hegemony, World Order and Historical Change: neo-Gramscian Perspectives in International Relations', *Capital and Class*, 82: 85–113.

Biersteker, T.J. 1989 'Critical Reflections on Post-Positivism in International Relations', *International Studies Quarterly*, 33 (3): 263–7.

Brown, C. 1992 *International Relations Theory: New Normative Approaches.* Toronto: Harvester Wheatsheaf.

Brown, C. 1994 'Turtles All the Way Down: Anti-Foundationalism, Critical Theory and International Relations', *Millennium: Journal of International Studies*, 23 (2): 213–36.

Bull, H. 1977 *Anarchical Society.* London: Macmillan.

Burnham, P. 1991 'Neo-Gramscian Hegemony and the International Order', *Capital and Class*, 45 (Fall): 73–93.

Burnham, P. 1999 'The Politics of Economic Management in the 1990s', *New Political Economy*, 4 (1): 37–54.

Carr, E.H. 1961 *What is History?* Harmondsworth: Penguin Books.

Cohen, B.J. 2007 'The transatlantic divide: Why are American and British IPE so different?', *Review of International Political Economy*, 14 (2): 197–219.

Cox, R.W. 1953 'The idea of international labor regulation', *International Labour Review*, 68 (2): 191–6. Reprinted in Cox, R.W. with T.J. Sinclair 1996 *Approaches to World Order.* Cambridge: Cambridge University Press.

Cox, R.W. 1969 'The executive head: an essay on leadership in international organization', *International Organization*, 23 (2): 205–30. Reprinted in Cox, R.W. with T.J. Sinclair 1996 *Approaches to World Order.* Cambridge: Cambridge University Press.

Cox, R.W. and J. Harrod, *et al.* 1972 *Future Industrial Relations: An Interim Report.* Geneva: International Institute for Labour Studies.

Cox, R.W. and Jacobson, H.K. 1972 *The Anatomy of Influence. Decision Making in International Organization.* New Haven: Yale University Press.

Cox, R.W. 1976 'On Thinking about Future World Order', *World Politics*, 28 (2): 175–96.

Cox, R.W. and Jacobson, H.K. 1977 'Decision making', *International Social Science Journal* (Special issue edited by Abi-Saab, G.), 29 (1): 115–35. Reprinted in Cox, R.W. with T.J. Sinclair 1996 *Approaches to World Order.* Cambridge: Cambridge University Press.

Cox, R.W. 1977 'Labor and Hegemony', *International Organization*, 31 (3): 385–424. Reprinted in Cox, R.W. with T.J. Sinclair 1996 *Approaches to World Order.* Cambridge: Cambridge University Press.

Cox, R.W. 1979 'Ideologies and the New International Economic Order: reflections on some recent literature', *International Organization*, 33 (2): 257–302. Reprinted in Cox, R.W. with T.J. Sinclair 1996 *Approaches to World Order.* Cambridge: Cambridge University Press.

Cox, R.W. 1980 'Labor and hegemony: a reply', *International Organization*, 34 (1): 159–76. Reprinted in Cox, R.W. with T.J. Sinclair 1996 *Approaches to World Order.* Cambridge: Cambridge University Press.

Cox, R.W. 1981 'Social Forces, States and World Orders: Beyond International Relations Theory', *Millennium: Journal of International Studies*, 10 (2): 126–55. Reprinted in Cox, R.W. with T.J. Sinclair 1996 *Approaches to World Order*. Cambridge: Cambridge University Press.

Cox, R.W. 1982 'Production and Hegemony: Toward a Political Economy of World Order', in Jacobson, H.K. and Sidjanski, D. (eds) *The Emerging International Economic Order: Dynamic Processes, Constraints, and Opportunities*. London: Sage Publications.

Cox, R.W. 1983 'Gramsci, Hegemony and International Relations: An Essay in Method', *Millennium: Journal of International Studies*, 12 (2): 162–75. Reprinted in Cox, R.W. with T.J. Sinclair 1996 *Approaches to World Order*. Cambridge: Cambridge University Press.

Cox, R.W. 1986 'Social Forces, States, and World Orders: Beyond International Relations Theory', with a Postscript (1985), in R.O. Keohane (ed.) *Neorealism and its Critics*. New York: Columbia University Press.

Cox, R.W. 1987 *Production, Power, and World Order: Social Forces in the Making of History*. New York: Columbia University Press.

Cox, R.W. 1989a 'Middlepowermanship, Japan, and future world order', *International Journal*, 44 (4): 823–62. Reprinted in Cox R.W. with T.J. Sinclair 1996 *Approaches to World Order*. Cambridge: Cambridge University Press.

Cox, R.W. 1989b 'Production, the State and Change in World Order', in Czempiel, E. and Rosenau, J.N. (eds) *Global Changes and Theoretical Challenges*. Toronto: Maxwell Macmillan.

Cox, R.W. 1992a 'Global Perestroika.' Reprinted in R.W. Cox with T.J. Sinclair 1996, *Approaches to World Order*. Cambridge: Cambridge University Press.

Cox, R.W. 1992b 'Towards a Post-Hegemonic Conceptualisation of World Order: Reflections on the Relevancy of Ibn Khaldun', in Rosenau, J.N. and Czempiel, E. (eds) *Governance without Government: Order and Change in World Politics*. Cambridge: Cambridge University Press.

Cox, R.W. 1992c 'Take six eggs': theory, finance, and the real economy in the work of Susan Strange', in R.W. Cox with T.J. Sinclair. *Approaches to World Order*. Cambridge: Cambridge University Press.

Cox, R.W. 1992d 'Multilateralism and World Order', *Review of International Studies*, 18 (2): 161–80.

Cox, R.W. 1993a 'The Global Political Economy and Social Choice', in Gill, S. (ed.) *Gramsci, Historical Materialism and International Relations*. Reprinted in Cox. R.W. with T.J. Sinclair 1996 *Approaches to World Order*. Cambridge: Cambridge University Press.

Cox, R.W. 1993b 'Structural Issues of Global Governance: Implications for Europe', in Gill, S. (ed.) *Gramsci, Historical Materialism and International Relations*. Cambridge: Cambridge University Press.

Cox, R.W. 1993c 'Production and Security', in Cox. R.W. with T.J. Sinclair. 1996 *Approaches to World Order*. Cambridge: Cambridge University Press.

Cox, R.W. 1993d 'Realism, Political Economy and the Future World', in Morgan, R. *et al.* (eds) *New Diplomacy in the Post-Cold War World: Essays for Susan Strange*. New York: St. Martin's Press.

Cox, R.W. 1995a 'Critical Political Economy', in Hettne, B. (ed.) *International Political Economy: Understanding Global Disorder*. London: Zed Books.

Cox, R.W. 1995b 'Civilizations: Encounters and Transformations', *Studies in Political Economy*, 47: 7–31.

Cox, R.W. with T.J. Sinclair 1996 *Approaches to World Order*. Cambridge: Cambridge University Press.

Cox, R.W. 1996a 'Civilisations in World Political Economy', *New Political Economy*, 1 (2): 141–54.

Cox, R.W. 1996b 'Influences and commitments', in R.W. Cox with T.J. Sinclair 1996 *Approaches to World Order*. Cambridge: Cambridge University Press.

Cox, R.W. 1996c 'A Perspective on Globalization', in Mittelman, J.H. (ed.) *Globalization: Critical Reflections*. London: Lynne Rienner.

Cox, R.W. 1996d 'Preface', in R.W. Cox with T.J. Sinclair 1996, *Approaches to World Order*. Cambridge: Cambridge University Press.

Cox, R.W. (ed.) 1997a *The New Realism: Perspectives on Multilateralism and World Order*. New York: United Nations University Press.

Cox, R.W. 1997b 'Some Reflections on the Oslo Symposium', in Gill, S. (ed.) *Globalization, Democratization and Multilateralism*. New York: United Nations University Press.

Cox, R.W. 1999a 'Civil society at the turn of the millenium: prospects for an alternative world order', *Review of International Studies*, 25 (1): 3–28.

Cox, R.W. (interview with R. Germain) 1999b 'The Millennium Symposium: Conversations with Manuel Castells, Robert Cox and Immanuel Wallerstein', *New Political Economy*, 4 (3): 379–408.

Cox, R.W. 1999c 'Susan Strange: A Personal Reflection', *BISA News: The Newsletter of the British International Studies Association*, nr 61 May 1999.

Cox, R.W. 2000 'Political Economy and World Order: Problems of Power and Knowledge at the Turn of the Millennium', in Stubbs, R. and Underhill, G.R.D. (eds) *Political Economy and the Changing Global Order (Second Edition)*. Ontario: Oxford University Press.

Cox, R.W. with Schechter, M. 2002 *The Political Economy of a Plural World: Critical Reflections on Power, Morals and Civilization*. London: Routledge.

Cox, R.W. 2004 'Beyond Empire and Terror: Critical Reflections on the Political Economy of World Order', *New Political Economy*, 9 (3): 307–23.

Devetak, R. 1996 'Critical Theory', in S. Burchill and A. Linklater (eds) *Theories of International Relations*. London: Macmillan Press.

Dickins, A. 2006 'The evolution of international political economy', *International Affairs*, 82 (3): 479–92.

Douglas, W.A. and Godson, R.S. 1980 'Labor and Hegemony: A Critique', *International Organization*, 34 (1): 149–58.

Eichengreen, B. 1996 *Globalizing Capital: A History of the International Monetary System*. Princeton: Princeton University Press.

Falk, R. 1997 'The critical realist tradition and the demystification of interstate power: E.H. Carr, Hedley Bull and Robert W. Cox', in S. Gill and J.H. Mittelman (eds) *Innovation and Transformation in International Studies*. Cambridge: Cambridge University Press.

Gamble, A. and Payne, A. (eds) 1996 *Regionalism and World Order*. Basingstoke, Hampshire: Macmillan.

George, J. 1989 'International Relations and the Search for Thinking Space: Another View of the Third Debate', *International Studies Quarterly*, 33 (3): 269–79.

George, J. 1994 *Discourses of Global Politics: A Critical (Re)Introduction to International Relations*. Boulder, Colorado: Lynne Rienner.

Germain, R.D. and Kenny, M. 1998 'Engaging Gramsci: International Relations Theory and the New Gramscians', *Review of International Studies*, 24 (1): 3–21.

Germain, R.D. 1999 'Review Essay. In Search of Political Economy: Understanding European Monetary Union', *Review of International Political Economy*, 6 (3): 390–8.

Germain, R.D. 2005 *Conceptualizing Global Financial Governance: An Essay in Method*. Unpublished paper.

Gill, S. 1990 *American Hegemony and the Trilateral Commission*. New York: Cambridge University Press.

Gill, S. (ed.) 1993a *Gramsci, Historical Materialism and International Relations*. Cambridge: Cambridge University Press.

Gill, S. 1993b 'Epistemology, ontology, and the "Italian School"'. In Gill, S. (ed.) *Gramsci, Historical Materialism and International Relations*. Cambridge: Cambridge University Press.

Gill, S. (ed.) 1997 *Globalization, Democratization and Multilateralism*. New York: United Nations University Press.

Gill, S. 2003 *Power and Resistance in the New World Order*. New York: Palgrave Macmillan.

Gill, S. and Mittelman, J.H. (eds) 1997 *Innovation and Transformation in International Studies*. Cambridge: Cambridge University Press.

Griffiths, M. 1999 *Fifty Key Thinkers in International Relations*. New York: Routledge.

Haacke, J. 1996 'Theory and Praxis in International Relations: Habermas, Self-Reflection, Rational Argumentation', *Millennium: Journal of International Studies*, 25 (2): 255–89.

Haas, E.B. 1964 *Beyond the Nation-State: Functionalism and International Organization*. Stanford: Stanford University Press.

Habermas, J. 1972 *Knowledge and Human Interests*. London: Heinemann.

Habermas, J. 1976 *Legitimation Crisis*. London: Heinemann.

Harrod, J. 1987 *Power, Production and the Unprotected Worker*. New York: Columbia University Press.

Held, D. 1980 *Introduction to Critical Theory: Horkheimer to Habermas*. Cambridge: Polity Press.

Hill, C. 1999 '"Where are we Going?" International Relations and the voice from below', *Review of International Studies*, 25 (1): 107–22.

Hoffman, M. 1987 'Critical Theory and the Inter-Paradigm Debate', *Millennium: Journal of International Studies*, 16 (2): 231–49.

Hoffman, M. 1988 'Conversations on Critical International Relations Theory', *Millennium: Journal of International Studies*, 17 (1): 91–5.

Hoffman, M. 1991 'Restructuring, Reconstruction, Reinscription, Rearticulation: Four Voices in Critical International Theory', *Millennium: Journal of International Studies*, 20 (2): 169–85.

Holsti, K.J. 1989 'Mirror, Mirror on the Wall, Which are the Fairest Theories of All?', *International Studies Quarterly*, 33 (3): 255–61.

Horkheimer, M. 1947 *Eclipse of Reason*. New York: Oxford University Press.

Horkheimer, M. (translated by O'Connell, M.J. and others) 1972 *Critical Theory: Selected Essays*. New York: The Seabury Press.

Jackson, R. and Sørensen, G. 1999 *Introduction to International Relations*. Oxford: Oxford University Press.

Kellner, D. 1989 *Critical Theory, Marxism and Modernity*. Cambridge: Polity Press.

Keohane, R.O. and Nye, J.S. (eds) 1971 *Transnational Relations and World Politics*. Massachusetts: Harvard University Press.

Keohane, R.O. and Nye, J.S. 1974 'Transgovernmental Relations and International Organizations', *World Politics*, 27 (1): 39–62.

Keohane, R.O. and Nye, J.S. 1977 *Power and Interdependence: World Politics in Transition*. Boston: Little Brown.

Keohane, R.O. 1981 'The Theory of Hegemonic Stability and Changes in International Economics Regimes, 1967–77', in O. Holsti, R. Siverson and A. George (eds) *Change in the International System*. Boulder: Westview Press.

Keohane, R.O. (ed.) 1986 *Neorealism and its Critics*. New York: Columbia University Press.

Keyman, E.F. 1997 *Globalization, State, Identity/Difference: Toward A Critical Social Theory of International Relations*. New Jersey: Humanities Press.

Kubalkova, V. and Cruickshank, A.A. 1986 'The 'New Cold War' in 'critical International Relations studies', *Review of International Studies*, 12 (3): 163–85.

Lapid, Y. 1989a 'The Third Debate: On the Prospects of International Theory in a Post-Positivist Era', *International Studies Quarterly*, 33 (3): 235–54.

Lapid, Y. 1989b 'Qua Vadis International Relations? Further Reflections on the 'Next Stage' of International Theory', *Millennium: Journal of International Studies*, 18 (1): 77–88.

Leysens, A.J. 2006 'Social Forces in Southern Africa: Transformation from Below?', *Journal of Modern African Studies*, 44 (1): 31–58.

Linklater, A. 1986 'Realism, Marxism and critical international theory', *Review of International Studies*, 12 (4): 301–12.

Linklater, A. 1990 *Beyond Realism and Marxism: Critical Theory and International Relations*. London: Macmillan.

Linklater, A. 1992 'International Relations Theory: A Critical-Theoretical Point of View', *Millennium: Journal of International Studies*, 21 (1): 77–98.

Linklater, A. 1998 *The Transformation of Political Community*. Columbia: University of South Carolina Press.

Marcuse, H. 1941 (reprint, 1977) *Reason and Revolution*. London: Routledge and Kegan Paul.

Madeuf, B. and Michalet, C. 1978 'A New Approach to International Economics', *International Social Science Journal*, 30 (2): 253–83.

Mittelman, J.H. 1998 'Coxian Historicism as an Alternative Perspective in International Studies', *Alternatives*, 23 (1): 63–92.

Mittelman, J.H. 2000 *The Globalization Syndrome: Transformation and Resistance*. Princeton, New Jersey: Princeton University Press.

Morgenthau, H.J. 1948 *Politics Among Nations: The Struggle for Power and Peace*. New York: Knopf.

Morgenthau, H.J. 1951 *In Defence of the National Interest*. New York: Knopf.

Morrow, R.A. with Brown, D.D. 1994 *Critical Theory and Methodology*. London: Sage.

Morse, E.L. 1976 *Modernization and the Transformation of International Relations*. New York: The Free Press.

Murphy, C.N. and Augelli, E. 1988 *America's Quest for Supremacy and the Third World: A Gramscian Analysis*. London: Pinter Publishers.

Murphy, C.N. and Tooze, R. (eds) 1991 *The New International Political Economy*. Boulder, CO: Lynne Rienner.

Murphy, C.N. 1994 *International Organization and Industrial Change*. Oxford: Oxford University Press.

Murphy, C.N. 1998 'Understanding IR: understanding Gramsci', Review of International Studies, 24 (3): 417–25.

Murphy, C.N. and Nelson, D. 2001 'A tale of two heterodoxies', *British Journal of Politics and International Relations*, 3 (3): 393–412.

Murphy, C.N. 2007 'The Promise of critical IR, partially kept', *Review of International Studies*, 33 (1): 1–17.

Neufeld, M.A. 1992 'The Pedagogical is Political: The 'Why', the 'What', and the 'How' in the Teaching of World Politics', in L.S. Gonick and E. Weisband (eds) *Teaching World Politics: Contending Pedagogies for a New World Order*. Boulder: Westview Press.

Neufeld, M.A. 1993a 'Reflexivity and International Relations Theory', *Millennium: Journal of International Studies*, 22 (1): 53–76.

Neufeld, M.A. 1993b 'Interpretation and the Science of International Relations', *Review of International Studies*, 19 (1): 39–61.

Neufeld, M.A. 1995 *The Restructuring of International Relations Theory*. Cambridge: Cambridge University Press.

Hoogvelt, A. Kenny, M. and Germain, R. 1999 'The Millennium Symposium: Conversations with Manuel Castells, Robert Cox and Immanuel Wallerstein'. *New Political Economy*, 4 (3): 379–408.

Pasha, M.K. 1997 'Ibn Khaldun and World Order', in Gill, S. and Mittelman, J.H. (eds) *Innovation and Transformation in International Studies*. Cambridge: Cambridge University Press.

Phillips, N. 2005a '"Globalizing" the Study of International Political Economy', in Phillips, N. (ed.) *Globalizing International Political Economy*. Basingstoke: Palgrave Macmillan.

Phillips, N. 2005b 'Globalization Studies in International Political Economy', in Phillips, N. (ed.) *Globalizing International Political Economy*. Basingstoke: Palgrave Macmillan.

Phillips, N. 2005c 'Wither IPE?', in Phillips, N. (ed.) *Globalizing International Political Economy*. Basingstoke: Palgrave Macmillan.

Polanyi, K. 1957 *The Great Transformation: The Political and Economic Origins of Our Time*. Boston: Beacon Press.

Rengger, N.J. 1988 'Going Critical? A Response to Hoffman', *Millennium: Journal of International Studies*, 17 (1): 81–9.

Rengger, N. and Hoffman, M. 1992 'Modernity, Post-Modernism and International Relations', in J. Doherty, E. Graham and M. Malek (eds) *Post-Modernism in the Social Sciences*. Houndmills, Basingstoke: Macmillan.

Schechter, M.G. 2002 'Critiques of Coxian Theory: Background to a Conversation', in R.W. Cox with M.G. Schechter. *The Political Economy of a Plural World: Critical Reflections on Power, Morals and Civilization*. London: Routledge.

Schmitter, P.C. 1974 'Still the Century of Corporatism?', in F.B. Pike and T. Stritch (eds) *The New Corporatism: Social-Political Structures in the Iberian World*. Notre Dame: University of Notre Dame Press.

Scholte, J.A. 2005 *Globalization: A Critical Introduction (second edition)*. London: Palgrave.

Sinclair, T.J. 1996 'Beyond international relations theory: Robert W. Cox and approaches to world order', in R.W. Cox with T.J. Sinclair. *Approaches to World Order*. Cambridge: Cambridge University Press.

Smith, S. 1995 'The Self-Images of a Discipline: A Genealogy of International Relations Theory', in S. Booth and S. Smith (eds) *International Relations Theory Today*. Pennsylvania: Pennsylvania State University Press.

Strange, S. 1988a 'Review of Production, Power and World Order: Social Forces in the Making of History', *International Affairs*, 64 (2) (Spring): 269–70.

Strange, S. 1988b *States and Markets: An Introduction to International Political Economy*. London: Pinter Publishers.

Taylor, I. 2001 *Stuck in Middle GEAR: South Africa's Post-Apartheid Foreign Relations*. London: Praeger.

Taylor, I. 2003 'Hegemony, Neo Liberal "Good Governance" and the International Monetary Fund: A Gramscian Perspective', in Bøås, M. and McNeill, B.D. (eds) *The Role of Ideas in Multinational Institutions*. New York: Routledge.

Thompson, I.L. (ed.) 2007 *Participatory Governance? Citizens and the State in South Africa*. Bellville: African Centre for Citizenship and Democracy.

Vasquez, J.A. 1995 'The Post-Positivist Debate: Reconstructing Scientific Enquiry and International Relations Theory After Enlightenment's Fall', in S. Booth and S. Smith (eds) *International Relations Theory Today*. Pennsylvania: Pennsylvania State University Press.

Van der Pijl, K. 1998 *Transnational Classes and International Relations*. London: Routledge.

Walker, R.B.J. 1988 *One World, Many Worlds: Struggles for a Just World Peace*. Boulder: Lynne Rienner.

Walker, R.B.J. 1989 'History and Structure in the Theory of International Studies', *Millennium: Journal of International Studies*, 18 (2): 163–83.

Walker, R.B.J. 1993 *Inside/Outside: International Relations as Political Theory*. Cambridge: Cambridge University Press.

Wallerstein, I. 1974 *The Modern World-System. Capitalist Agriculture and the Origins of the European World-Economy in the Sixteenth Century*. New York: Academic Press.

Wallerstein, I. 1976 *The Modern World System* (volumes 1 and 2). Beverly Hills: Sage.

Wallerstein, I. 1979 *The Capitalist World Economy*. Cambridge: Cambridge University Press.

Waltz, K.N. 1979 *Theory of International Politics*. London: Addison-Wesley.

Wyn Jones, R. 2001 'Introduction', in R. Wyn Jones (ed.) *Critical Theory and World Politics*. Boulder: Lynne Rienner.

Index